packaging
the news

D1637192

packaging
the news

A CRITICAL SURVEY OF
PRESS, RADIO, TV

by JAMES ARONSON

INTERNATIONAL PUBLISHERS
New York

For

LOUIS E. BURNHAM

and his bright memory

Library of Congress Catalog Card Number: 72-150662
SBN 7178-0317-1
Printed in the United States of America

Contents

1

In the beginning . . .

THE FIRST year of the decade of the 1970's might well be termed a Time of the Toad for the communications industry. It was a time of frontal government assaults on the integrity and credibility of the press and the television networks under the field generalship of the Vice President, but with the Commander in Chief issuing the directives from the White House.

It was a time also of government subpoenas for the working press, and for newspapers, newsmagazines, and the television networks themselves; of reporters and photographers turning up as agents of the FBI on the home front, and of the CIA on the foreign fronts; of Army counterintelligence operatives being accredited as newspaper correspondents in Vietnam to snoop on legitimate reporters. And, as any sensitive reporter at a demonstration in Foley Square in New York or Market Street in San Francisco could tell you, that good-looking chap in the trench coat, looking terribly Front Page behind his crisp new press badge, might well be one of J. Edgar Hoover's boys out for a little look-see, or the man from the local police Red Squad. In any case, no one ever saw him before, or ever heard of the New Suburbia News Agency listed on his press badge.

It was a time that was forcing decisions in the communications industry—from top to bottom. For

the owners and operators of the media, the decision
was whether to resist, individually and collectively,
a direct encroachment on the freedom of the press
by the national Administration; or whether to ac-
cede to the pressures and demands behind a dust
storm of indignant rhetoric and double talk. For the
men and women who work for the newspapers and
the radio-television networks, the decision was
whether to comply or to determine the extent to
which they could use their power to persuade their
employers to resist and, if persuasion failed, the
extent to which they would use their own power to
counter their employers' capitulation.

These were pressing questions in a time of increasingly serious repression of dissent within
America against the policies of the government of
the United States—internal and external. It is
against this present-day setting that the intent of the
framers of the Bill of Rights must be gauged and, in
turn, the actions of the government and the owners
and operators of the communications media interpreted.

The men who drew up the First Amendment
guarantee of the freedom of the press could hardly
have envisioned the vast expansion of communications in the nation and the world in the second half
of the 20th century. Yet their 18th century parch-
ment was written with a philosophical and practical
foresight which remains valid today.

When they insisted that Congress shall make no
law abridging the freedom of the press, they were
not attempting to erect unscalable walls around the
newspapers of the day which served mainly local
needs and the interests of the cities on the eastern
seaboard. They sought to guarantee that the press
would be free to criticize government without fear
of reprisal, that it would speak and crusade in the

public interest against any established authority which might seek to abrogate the rights of the public. At its core, the First Amendment sought to guarantee that the government could not censor the press, but that the press should, for all time, have the right—indeed that it was duty bound—to censor government.

This principle was operative for the press even before the success of the Revolution, and the contribution of the forthright newspapers of the day in the establishment of the Republic cannot be overestimated. The commitment of the editors to freedom persisted into the post-Revolutionary era which saw the first contests between press and government—as well as the first attempts at management of the news. President Washington, stung by criticism in the press, denounced the offending newspapers as scurrilous and irresponsible, thus establishing a precedent which has been followed by every succeeding President.

A kind of wild abandon marked the newspapers of the early 19th century. They were almost always individually owned and operated, and the mark of the editor-publisher was ever present, often erratic, partisan, and violent, but almost always stimulating. There occurred at the time a remarkable increase in the number of newspapers, allowing for a great diversity of opinion. In the United States in 1830, there were more newspapers with a greater readership than in any other country in the world. Quality varied, but politics was omnipresent and dominated the contents of the press.

The question of slavery increasingly became a subject of passionate debate and, as would be the requirement henceforth in American journalism, the most passionate believers and dissenters were forced to establish and finance their own journals.

Thus, in 1821, in Mount Pleasant, Ohio, William Lundy began his *Genius of Universal Emancipation,* with no capital and with only six subscribers.[1] He would walk to Steubenville, which reemerged briefly in the news 149 years later as the most unhealthy city in the nation, to get his paper printed, and return with the edition on his back. For his passion, he was almost beaten to death in Baltimore by a slave dealer, but he persevered until 1855. In 1831, William Lloyd Garrison founded *The Liberator* in Boston where, for 34 years, it was the most courageous and effective of the anti-slavery papers. In a preview of the debate over withdrawal of troops from Vietnam, Garrison was for immediate abolition of slavery, while Lundy was a gradualist.

Garrison was beaten by mobs in Boston, and the plants of several anti-slavery papers (including John Greenleaf Whittier's *Pennsylvania Freeman* in Philadelphia) were wrecked. The worst violence occurred in Alton, Illinois, in 1837, with the murder of the Reverend Elijah P. Lovejoy, a journalist turned Presbyterian minister. He had moved his *Observer* plant across the river from St. Louis in the hope of finding greater freedom, but the shop was wrecked three times. As he sought to rebuild it for the fourth time, the building was attacked again and he was shot to death.

The abolitionist papers never achieved large circulations, and their refusal to compromise their radical views alienated the liberals of the time. But they succeeded in their gadfly role and pricked the conscience of the Northern press, forcing many publishers to look up from their profit sheets long enough to note that the institution of slavery violated all concepts of freedom on which the Republic had been founded less than a century before. It is instructive for today's radicals (and their detractors, who nonetheless regard Garrison as an American hero) that Garrison was the leader of a group of non-compromisers who advocated civil disobedience to the fugitive slave laws, and who refused to acknowledge court decisions upholding slaveowners' rights to reclaim runaways.

At mid-century the invention of the telegraph revolutionized the newspaper industry, and this, along with technological improvement in printing and press work, brought about significant changes in the content and appearance of the newspapers, and a break with the parochialism which derived in part from lack of communication.

In the post-Civil War era, and particularly in the last two decades of the 19th century, the American press was transformed from an individualistic entrepreneur medium into a sophisticated corporate entity in keeping with the phenomenal growth of the nation. The cities were expanding, more people had money and wanted goods, and advertising became the medium for separating them from their money.

Competition was the key word in the newspaper industry, and the rush for profits frenzied. In 1880 in the United States, there were 850 newspapers in the English language; in 1890 there were 1,967. And both new and old began to identify their publications more closely with the business community. The class approach became dominant. If the press became more "responsible" by printing a wider range of news in greater detail and less individual partisanship, the responsibility was nonetheless selective, and it often paralleled the publishers' identification with the national interest, as interpreted by the expanding capitalist class. This in turn led to a decrease in critical editorial comment about government and industry.

The influence of newspapers was great. Many of

them were marked by a rabid sensationalism which
became known as "yellow journalism." A classic
example of yellow journalism was the propaganda
war which William Randolph Hearst and Joseph
Pulitzer declared against Spain, preparing the public
for the actual declaration of war by President
McKinley and the Congress in 1898.

2

Nothing to gain but their chains

IN THE first decade of the 20th century, newspapers
were bought and sold with the frenzy of stock
market speculation, and the newspaper chains (they
are now tidily called "groups") began their spectacular rise. In the course of his swashbuckling career
from populist socialism to jingoist reaction, Hearst,
for example, established or purchased 42 newspapers. After the wholesale manipulation, swapping
and merging, came the paring down process, which
has continued into the current journalistic scene—a
time that has been termed the era of the vanishing
newspaper.

Personal journalism went out with World War II,
and in its place—except in a few instances—came
disengaged journalism, with bloodless men in the
publishers' chairs and the editors' sanctums. This
disengaged, or so-called objective, journalism became an unwritten code for the news staff, but not
for the editorial writers. Even in the news columns

it imposed strictures on reporters and rewrite men which resulted in weighting stories (in the name of fairness) in favor of the status quo, and tipping the scales against those who advocated political and social change, or who were the victims of reaction.

The modern philosophy of the newspaper industry espoused by chain publishers like S. I. Newhouse, James S. Copley, and John H. Perry, was expressed most succintly by Lord Roy Thomson, Canadian born, whose invasion of the United States has left some publishers a bit apprehensive. "It is the business of newspapers," said Thomson, "to make money."

This slogan, flashing in neon lights over batteries of electronic computers and new web offset presses with which the American press has belatedly entered the modern world, is the inspiration in the front offices of almost every newspaper from coast to coast. And in 1970, there were 1,758 daily newspapers (442 fewer than the peak of 2,200 in 1900— but infinitely more profitable).

The highest mortality rate among newspapers has been in the large cities. Where once there were 14 dailies in New York and eight in Boston, there are now three in each city. Yet the total number of newspapers has remained virtually unchanged since the end of World War II. The surface stability is accounted for in the rise of suburban newspapers, some with circulations of half a million.

Despite the prevailing impression of the seemingly disappearing newspaper, and the belief that television advertising has cut into newspaper revenue, the newspaper industry is doing very well indeed. The conglomerates—a new form of monopoly— have paid off handsomely by cutting costs through mergers, pared down staffs and package deals offered by newspapers under the same ownership in one city, or in a group of cities. In 1969 advertising revenues (the main source of newspaper profits) amounted to $5.4 billion, or 22 per cent more than the total for radio and television combined.[2]

But the most startling journalism statistic today is that out of 1,500 cities of the United States with daily newspapers, only 45 have competing newspapers under separate ownership. What this does to freedom of choice in the news and to diversity of opinion—however limited it may have been before—is self-evident. Thus, about 63 million Americans each day—10 million more than in 1948, when there were 30 more papers—are reading fewer papers and fewer points of view than ever before.

While the spread of syndication and the growth of wire services have brought expanded coverage into previously news-blighted areas, the ratio of news as against advertising in the daily press is 40 per cent to 60 per cent, an almost exact reversal of the pre-World War II press.

The press of America, with a few notable exceptions, is marked by a prefabricated standardization of news which is constricting and depressing. Newspapers seem to come from a colossal sausage machine which grinds out words in digestible packages to suit each region of the nation. The same commentators appear in the newspapers coast to coast the same day—James Reston and Joseph Alsop, Jack Anderson and William F. Buckley Jr., cheek by jowl with the comic strips and the service columns, news features, advice to the lovelorn (with a mod gloss as a synthetic acknowledgment of the new sexual freedom), household hints, book reviews, and sports columns.

In many instances, the columnists have replaced or overshadowed vapid editorial opinion. In fact, many newspapers still publish "canned" editorials and political cartoons supplied by the syndicated word-and-pen factories whose products are generally so bland that they may be used word for word in papers with supposedly varying political points of view. The blandness is replaced by patriotic alarm when communism or law-and-order is the topic; but the serviceability of the editorials remains unimpaired because the American press, Democratic, Republican or "politically independent," speaks in one voice on these matters.

There has thus come into being an unofficial and loosely associated national news network which in one way or another affects every newspaper in the country. It tends to insure that all persons who read newspapers will be similarly influenced by the news and commentary they absorb daily. It follows that they will think alike, and their thinking will be encouraged to defend the "national interest." The national interest is interpreted for them by the managers of the syndicates and the owners of the newspapers—businessmen who identify themselves, because of their conglomerate financial concerns, with national policies which protect these financial concerns, including investment in huge war manufacturing plants sweetly described as defense industries.

For these proprietors, newspapers are no longer entities in themselves, with individual character, courage, and a dedication to the public service, but simply properties to be listed among their holdings along with real estate, fertilizer, electronics, and aerospace rocketry. Unlike fertilizers, however, newspapers deal with information, ideas, and opinions that ought to help people understand and shape national policies. The economic centralization of newspapers, along with the rest of industry, is a disastrous departure from what once was known in town hall forums as the free exchange of ideas in the marketplace of public opinion.

The evil of bigness in itself may be debatable, but the dangers of monopoly news and monopoly opinion-making are not. This conformity is most striking in the commitment of the press to the American way of life under capitalism. For its owners, any other way is equated with sin and deviltry—although in the last years, particularly since the emergence of differences among socialist countries, some publishers and editors purport to see a glimmer of hope that socialism is not the monolithic enemy they once feared; that there is a chance that some socialist governments may see the light and move into the "free world" as shaped by the makers and administrators of American foreign policy, an example of which is Vietnam.

Within the concept propagated by the owners of the newspaper industry, publishers, editors, reporters, and commentators enjoy complete freedom of the press and may say what they will. This includes criticism of governmental methods and practices, legislation before the Congress or local legislatures, investigations of corruption in high places (rare, but still undertaken), generalized reporting and editorializing about pollution and destruction of natural resources, concern over fluctuating social and moral values—all of these things, but never basic criticism of or opposition to national policies.

Despite the self-imposed restrictions of this concept, the content of some newspapers and the scope of their coverage have improved. The *Los Angeles Times* is a case in point. Although it is still essentially the spokesman for business and farm monopolies throughout Southern California, in the last decade it has broadened both its news policies and editorial positions to the point where, in June 1970, under the impact of widespread opposition to the war, it actually advocated United States withdrawal from Vietnam, "swiftly, and without equivocation."

It set a timetable of 18 months, but said the withdrawal must be "total and orderly." And while its recommendation in general was commendable, its general position nonetheless reaffirmed its devotion to basic American policy: unremitting hostility to communism. "Our great adversary is now, and will remain, the Soviet Union," it said in the same editorial. "We shall be engaged against the Communist world in one way or another all our lives." Underscoring this view was its indorsement of the reelection of Ronald Reagan as governor of California in November 1970.

While the reader of the *Los Angeles Times* must pick his way through a forest of ads for swimming pools and geriatric medical aids in his hunt for news and commentary, he will find both in greater profusion than ever before, and often presented with considerable enlightenment. The *Times,* however, has made no sacrifices in expanding its news coverage. It has grown fatter and richer than ever. In seemingly perverse fashion, also, its growing affluence may be traced to its increasing acceptance of a reality which has been forced upon it and other improving American newspapers—the impact of television news.

3

The all-seeing screen

MILLIONS OF Americans today get their news almost exclusively from television and from radio, particularly all-news radio in major urban centers which broadcast news 24 hours a day. We no longer see the world from the perspective of the earth itself, as anthropologist Margaret Mead said recently: we now see the earth itself from the moon. More precisly, television has, for example, brought the war in Indochina, with all its indigestible awfulness, to the American dinner table for the six o'clock news, and repeated it on the 10 or 11 o'clock news for waking nightmares.

No one is more acutely aware of this impact than President Nixon and his chief pro-consul, Vice President Agnew, who prowls the land on a long White House leash, to persuade the citizenry that they never saw what they had just seen, and if they insist they did see it, they should not believe it anyway. There will be more later about Agnew and the relationship of the media to the government.

In the decade of the 1960's, there is no question that television became the single most important medium in the United States. There is unanimity on this view among advertisers (even though the larger share of the advertising dollar still goes to the print medium), surveys like the Roper poll (which reported that the public trusts television news more than newspaper reports) and theorists like Marshall

McLuhan (for whom style and form are more important than content). In his book, *Television, A World View,* Wilson Dizard (Syracuse University Press, 1966) declared that television, more than any other medium, has the ability to identify and define our environment.

There are today, as there have been for many years, three major TV and radio networks, NBC, CBS, and ABC, each network owning and operating about 15 stations. There are, in addition, about 700 so-called independent TV stations, and 6,300 radio stations, for a total of more than 7,000 commercial broadcasting outlets. Many of the "independents" are affiliated with larger groups like Metromedia and Westinghouse Group W. All the stations (but not the networks) are licensed by the Federal Communications Commission for a period of three years. In addition, the FCC grants licenses and renewals to some five million transmitters, according to Elizabeth Drew in the *Atlantic Monthly.* These include radio, television, marine, police, fire, industrial, transportation, amateur outlets, and common carrier. About 800,000 licenses are processed each year for renewal.

Remarkably enough, the *Atlantic Monthly* reported in July 1969, in a survey of the ownership and influence of the "media moguls," as it called them, "there is no single government agency which has made it its business to assemble all the data on the reaches of this country's most powerful communicators in usable form." This included not only radio and television, but newspapers, magazines, book publishers and recording companies as well.

One reason for the casual bookkeeping is that neither the owners and operators of the communications media, nor their friends in high government places want the public to know, for example, that as of three years ago, there were 73 communities in the country in which all the newspapers and broadcasting facilities were owned by one man or one corporation.

The FCC, which keeps the most complete records in certain areas, reported in November 1968 that daily newspapers owned outright or had a controlling interest in the licenses of 640 broadcasting stations, out of a total of 6,800. Of these, 303 were AM stations, 189 FM stations, and 148 television stations.

Speaking of the broadcasting power of the big networks themselves, FCC Commissioner Nicholas Johnson, the most outspoken member of the commission, described in his book *How to Talk Back to Your Television Set* (Atlantic Monthly Press, 1970) how they freeze out the possibility of local ownership by means of group control. Under this method, the controlling group bargains with networks, advertisers, and talent with offers that place the smaller individual stations at a disadvantage. But above all, Johnson warned in his book: "The national political power involved in ownership of a group of major VHF television stations in, say, New York, Los Angeles, Philadelphia, and Washington, D.C., is greater than a democracy should unthinkingly repose in one man or corporation."

There are times when an event must be covered live and unedited, simply because of its unavoidable urgency and news appeal. Its impact may come into conflict with the basic desire both of government and the owners of the communications media to mute or manipulate the event itself.

One such event was the first visit to the United States of Soviet Prime Minister Nikita Khrushchev in 1959, which I observed firsthand as part of the incredible and often incredulous press horde that accompanied the Soviet visitor and his host, United Nations Ambassador Henry Cabot Lodge, from New York to Los Angeles and back across the country. The event was overwhelming both in itself and its impact on the people of the United States. As an example of Cold War journalism, it was a classic.

Immediately following the announcement of President Eisenhower's invitation to Khrushchev, full-page ads blossomed in the daily press urging a "National Day of Mourning." Editorials in the *New York Times* and the *Washington Post* warned the public to beware of Khrushchev's "effort at brainwashing," and "to make propaganda and sow the seeds of dissension."

There was saturation coverage of the visit in the press, much of it ranging in the early stages from unkind to vicious. Khrushchev was given a "waddle" rather than a walk, his wife's dresses drew derisive comments from Hearst's fashion reporters. There was even an unsubtle discussion of assassination possibilities by syndicated columnist Jim Bishop.

Newspapermen have always been known for their skepticism and cynicism—much of it warranted—but on the Khrushchev trip many of them ranged from unbalanced objectivity into the realm of active opposition, in person and in print. They made no effort to conceal their hostility, and yet there was a curious quality to the hostility: it was as if they were adopting this conforming attitude because each thought the other expected it of them.

There was, however, a new element to the coverage: television. For the first time in their own country—except for United Nations events—Americans by the millions were spectators at an international occasion whose potential for world peace was overwhelming—and they sensed it immediately. Despite years of conditioning and warning against the "international communist conspiracy," the American public was curious about this man from Moscow (which heretofore had been synonymous with Mars), and what they saw of him, his family, and his colleagues roused a spirit of indignation against the newspapers which were presenting the visit in a manner which bore little resemblance to what they were seeing. This spirit was reflected in a flood of letters to the editor in newspapers across the country, and its impact on the working press was demonstrated in the changing quality of their reports, particularly after spectacular welcomes for the Russians at several railroad stops en route from Los Angeles to San Francisco.

It was not a matter of Americans becoming captivated by an encounter with a representative of socialism. It was a deeply-felt expression of their hope and yearning for an end to bitterness and hostility between the two nations, and a desire for peace. The wounds of Korea had hardly closed, and there were ominous rumbles of impending American involvement in Southeast Asia. While the editors of the *New York Times* and the *Washington Post* would protest indignantly if they were charged with seeking to dampen these hopes, it was clear that they were committed to the Cold War, and sought to enlist the public in this commitment. Some were less subtle than others. The *San Francisco Examiner,* on September 22, 1959, started off its lead story on the visit in this fashion:

Fast-talking Nikita Khrushchev carried his good-will sales campaign to San Francisco yesterday, still acting more like a peace-loving peasant than the most dangerous man in history.

James Reston, who covered the journey at a comfortable distance from the sweltering horde of reporters, was far less crude than the *Examiner,* but his approach was not dissimilar. In an analytical article in the *New York Times* on September 24, 1959, he deplored the "smothering" coverage of the event and determined that it gave the visitor no pain. Reston wrote:

He is less interested in seeing America than in having the world see him in America, and for this purpose the reporters, photographers, technicians and all their gear are not only useful but indispensable. Millions of feet of film have been taken of this astonishing odyssey. If it were all put together it would produce a remarkably accurate but devastating record of the "new diplomacy." It will be interesting to see what comes out in Africa and Asia when the Soviet propagandists get through cutting the film record to size and shape.

You can bet your last ruble that it will show Mr. Khrushchev getting an enthusiastic welcome. Whoever said that pictures do not lie is the biggest liar of all, for this film can be made to show anything. The silent crowds can be eliminated and the applauding crowds can be retained. . . . In a world-wide propaganda battle, this is not frivolous nonsense. It is deadly serious.

Reston stated the problem from the point of view of American diplomacy, with which he closely identified himself—to the point of giving Lodge and the State Department some sound advice about altering their clumsy handling of the arrangements for the visit. It would of course have been in the interests of American policy to show to the world an America polite but cool to Khrushchev, united behind Administration policy in the face of this formidable challenge by world socialism's then current chief representative.

But this could not be honestly reported because this was not what happened. That fact perhaps was what troubled Reston most and created a problem for him—and for Washington. Indeed it was a problem. The people of America were, remarkably, far more interested in getting past the picture of socialism and its leaders which had been presented to them for years by their elected and appointed officials, and the communications industry. Contrary to Reston's contention, pictures do not lie. The truth was that television had added an entirely new and vital dimension to the coverage of news.

The danger (to American foreign policy) of the visit was underscored by the result of a Gallup poll taken September 28, immediately after Khrushchev's departure. The question asked was: "All things considered, do you think Khrushchev's visit to the United States has been a good thing or a bad thing?" The answers: good thing, 52 per cent; bad think, 19 per cent; neutral or no opinion, 29 per cent.

The operators of the television networks, apparently appalled at what they had wrought, set about at once to work on that 52 per cent. Teams of experts were gathered to discuss the visit, and no aspect of the tour was too large or too small for disparagement: the Premier's personality ("unstable and emotional"); his world disarmament proposal before the United Nations Assembly ("unrealistic and utopian"); his approach to the American farm and business communities ("Machiavellian"). The urgency of the counterattack demonstrated the concern of government and the com munications industry that an alteration of the Soviet image in the eyes of the American public would inevitably raise questions about United States foreign policy and, logically, a demand for changes in that policy.

4

Management and acquiescence

I HAVE dwelt at such length on the Khrushchev experience because it was perhaps the first major episode, involving television, in the widening debate concerning the communications media, its relationship to government, and its responsibility to the public. The debate has continued through the years of war in Indochina, the rise of a militant black freedom movement, and the shifting tides of the young white radical movement, and has focused on the violence in all three areas. It has brought into the open, among other things, the steady efforts by the national administrations, whether Republican or Democratic, to manage the news as completely as it can. It has also exposed the ambivalence of the communications industry, whose owners waver between their sound news judgment and the responsibility which this judgment entails, and their identification with the so-called national interest which, too often, becomes in their minds indistinguishable from government policy.

On the government side, the campaign and the

style vary with the personalities of the leaders. Eisenhower himself was not a manipulator of the media. His prestige as the commander of the Allied forces in World War II allowed the hero image to persevere almost intact through his eight years in office. The press was both forgiving and protective of his numerous demonstrations of ignorance and inadequacy in his statments on policy, and his subordinates in the adapted military chain of command which marked his Administration managed the media and their Washington representatives with conparative ease. Even Vice President Nixon did not break ranks, although his salivation as as he stood at attention was frequently evident.

John F. Kennedy was a master manipulator and coopter of the press. He not only called his favorite newspaper men in for confidential talks, but made unpublicized visits to their homes—unpublicized, that is, except at cocktail parties, where the honored host made certain that the visit was thoroughly publicized. Like all manipulators, Kennedy made his mistakes. In the Bay of Pigs in 1961, he persuaded the press, particularly the *New York Times,* to withhold information which, if it had been made public, might have raised against the Cuban adventure a public outcry great enough to have forced its abandonment. Then, when the adventure ended in failure, he first charged the press with having caused the failure, then later rebuked it for not disclosing the plans and preventing the acute governmental embarrassment.

He improved his techniques with time. In the confrontation with the Soviet Union in the missile crisis in October 1962, he managed a tighter rein on the press, and achieved the secrecy necessary for him to issue his ultimatum to the Soviet Union on the withdrawal of missiles from Cuban territory.

This self-imposed censorship by the communications industry—the *New York Times* and the *Washington Post* knew the details of the Kennedy strategy—prevented the issue from being brought before the United Nations in time to forestall a world-wide panic over the threat of nuclear war between the two great powers.

In both the Bay of Pigs episode and the missile crisis, the communications industry demonstrated lack of courage, lack of will, and an acquiescence in becoming a virtual arm of government.

Lyndon Johnson was not only a manipulator—he was a liar and bungler too. Where Kennedy took selected correspondents into his confidence, Johnson was moved by his overwhelming ego to impress upon the entire journalistic fraternity his unfailing statesmanship and political acumen. He alienated some of the correspondents from time to time, and forced them, for their own self-respect and credibility, to expose his misrepresentations and miscalculations. But in time of crisis, almost all of them got back in line. The fact that Johnson emerged from his time in office with as few scars as he did does not speak well for the communications media in general and the Washington press corps in particular. Even the now-it-can-be-told books about the Johnson years are defective in presenting the full grossness of the man and his relationship with the media.

The mark of the Nixon Administration in its relations with both the media and the public is a combination of duplicity, fraud, and polarizing pressure, all packaged in the slick Madison Avenue formula which carried Nixon to the Presidency, and all as synthetic—and as dangerous—as the man himself and the forces for whom he speaks.

There is no new or old Nixon. There has always

been only one: calculating, anxious, and supremely ambitious in the overcompensating manner of inadequate men. He has managed always, behind a facade of noxious sincerity, to pay off old scores when the power of his office afforded him an opportunity. His relations with the press, to the degree that the amenities and requirements of his position allow, follow this pattern.

Neither Nixon nor the correspondents who covered him have forgotten his bitter "farewell" press conference following his defeat for the governorship of California by Edmund G. Brown in November 1962. It is significant still because it reveals the unadorned and unpackaged Nixon, and it foretold—in somewhat contradictory fashion—what was to come. It was a long, rambling, self-serving statement that Nixon made, but the heart of it was in these sentences:

> As I leave the press, all I can say is this: for sixteen years, ever since the Hiss case, you've had a lot of fun—a lot of fun—that you've had an opportunity to attack me and I think I've given as good as I've taken. . . . I think it's time that our great newspapers have at least the same objectivity, the same fullness of coverage, that television has. And I can only say thank God for television and radio for keeping the newspapers a little more honest. . . . But as I leave you I want you to know—just think how much you're going to be missing. You won't have Nixon to kick around any more, because, gentlemen, this is my last press conference.

This last assertion, like so many subsequent Nixon comments, proved unfortunately to have no basis in fact. It could have remained a subject of high hilarity among newspaper people—if the Madison Avenue alchemy had not proved so effective in 1968.

It would of course be absurd to trace the current

governmental assault on the communications media to Nixon's bitterness in 1962 (although this element is present). It has far wider and more sinister implications. The inclusion of television is one major clue. Television served its purpose during the Presidential campaign, when the Nixon mechanics directed and stage-managed every one of his appearances on the medium. Now, however, except for the carefully contrived special-message appearances, and the somewhat less predictable "live" press conferences, Nixon must take his chances, as all other politicians do.

The Administration's attacks on the media, however, must be removed from the realm of personal Presidential politics to the realm of national and international policy, where it properly belongs.

5

No news is Agnews

THE OPENING gun in the assault on the media was fired in typically reverse Nixon style by Frank J. Shakespeare Jr., director of the U.S. Information Agency, in a speech on September 26, 1969, before the Radio-Television News Directors Association. He said: "You must fight against any effort by any government—that would make any effort (God knows I don't think the Nixon government would ever do it) to try to influence your judgments."

God knows, the Nixon Administration did do it, just six weeks after Shakespeare's fervent pronouncment, in the first of a series of speeches by

Vice President Agnew, in Des Moines. It was directed primarily at television and radio as the most vulnerable targets of news management through intimidation (control of licenses by the Federal Communications Commission). Agnew then proceeded to Birmingham to extend the assault to the press, primarily to the *New York Times* and the *Washington Post,* both critical of aspects of the Administration's foreign policy. Following are some excerpts from the speeches:

President Nixon's words and policies were subjected to instant analysis and querulous criticism.

We do know that to a man these commentators and producers live and work in the geographical and intellectual confines of Washington, D.C., and New York City. . . . We can deduce that these men read the same newspapers. They draw their political and social views from the same sources.

Is it not fair and relevant to question [TV news] concentration in the hands of a tiny enclosed fraternity of privileged men elected by no one? . . . As with other American institutions, perhaps it is time that the networks were made more responsive to the views of the nation and more responsible to the people they serve.

A single company, in the nation's capital, holds control of the largest newspaper in Washington, D.C., and one of the four major television stations, and an all-news radio station, and one of the three major news magazines—all grinding out the same editorial line.

The day when network commentators and even the gentlemen of the *New York Times* enjoyed a form of diplomatic immunity from comment and criticism of what they said . . . is over. The time for blind acceptance of their opinions is past.

I'm raising these questions so that the American people will become aware of—and think of the implications of—the growing monopoly that involves the voices of public opinion.

Agnew's charges were largely demagoguery and misrepresentations, but the threats were clear. The reference to the "instant analysis" of the President's significant November 3, 1969, speech, seeking to rally the "silent majority" to support his foreign policy, is an example. The speech actually was in the hands of reporters two hours before it was delivered, and they were in addition briefed by Presidential adviser Henry Kissinger before the speech was broadcast.

The attempt to mark the commentators and analysts as effete inhabitants of the Eastern seaboard was an appeal to "middle America" (as the real America) to reject them. And while Agnew was on solid ground in noting the growth of conglomerates in Washington as elsewhere (his reference was to the ownership by the Washington Post Company of a television and radio station in the capital, and of *Newsweek* magazine), his scope was limited to monopolies which opposed aspects of Administration policy. He might have noted other and larger conglomerates—the *Chicago Tribune* and *New York Daily News* combine, for example, the Gannett chain and the Copley chain; but these of course are supporters of the Nixon Administration. The Vice President's alliterative flourishes, which have become his trade mark, were more carefully researched and compiled than his facts and figures.

The assault, however, was carefully prepared and timed by the Administration, and it had a double purpose:

1. In the short range, to inhibit coverage of the November 15, 1969, mobilization in Washington and of anti-war demonstrations in general. The mobilization turned out to be the greatest convo-

cation for peace in the nation's history, but there
was no live coverage by any television network.
Variety, the weekly newspaper of the entertainment and communications industry, reported that
the networks had decided on their own in advance against live coverage. But the first Agnew
speech guaranteed that the decision would not be
reversed by an industry not noted for spine.

2. In the long range, to achieve by pressure and
threat of indirect control what the Administration
cannot do by legislation. The First Amendment
forbids the enactment of legislation abridging the
freedom of the press, but governmental harrass-
ment and intimidation can achieve the same
goals.

The Agnew attacks had three results:

1. A flurry of indignant and defiant editorials in
the nation's press—some of them of high quality—restating the constutional guarantees of the
freedom of the press; and statements by heads of
the television networks—of varying quality—
declaring in essence that the networks would not
be intimidated.

2. A sandstorm of telephone calls, letters, and
telegrams in support of the Agnew-Nixon position, indicating that the President's speech of
November 3 had been effective.

3. Evidence, in the volume and "balance" of
the coverage of the Agnew speeches and the
reaction to them, that the Administration had to a
great extent succeeded in its purpose of intimidation.

It is not accurate to label the new assaults on the
communications media as a *new McCarthyism,* any

more than it was completely accurate to character-
ize the repressive acts of the 1950's as *McCarthyism*. Neither the past efforts nor the present ones
stood any chance of success without the blessing of
the various Administrations—from Truman on
down through Nixon—or without the acquiescence
of the communications media, however troubled
that acquiescence may have been at times. In fact,
"McCarthyism" was government policy in the
1950's, just as "Agnewism" is in the 1970's.

It is significant that one day after the Shakespeare
address to the television directors, and six weeks
before the first Agnew speech, the September 27,
1969, issue of *TV Guide* noted that television news
and special events programs were undergoing significant changes. They were shifting away from
emphasis on the activities of the militant left, and
toward the center and the right. All three networks,
said the magazine, will be "exploring middle and
lower-middle class Americans."

In its issue of the same date, *Editor & Publisher,*
the weekly journal of the newspaper industry, said:
"The shift . . . is a reflection of the views of what is
called 'the silent majority' who feel television has
devoted too much time to the role of the militant
and the agitator and has given too little coverage to
the quiet hard-working Americans of all races."

It was not until five weeks later, November 3,
1969, that Nixon employed the phrase "the silent
majority" so effectively.

6

The man from Justice

IF THE purpose of the Agnew attacks was not clear to all, any confusion was dispelled by the great subpoena crusade of Attorney General John Mitchell, which followed. It was not so much to encourage the "silent majority" to expression as to render silent the majority of men and women who report, edit, and broadcast the news and commentary. In this strategy (as will be shown later), there was special emphasis on silencing particularly the growing number of black reporters in the general press where, until recently, there had been tokenism, or no blacks at all.

Involved in the subpoena affair was the increasingly sharp debate taking place in the world of journalism over the question of objectivity—whether, in an increasingly complex world, an intelligent and even dispassionate reporter could confine himself to reporting the facts objectively, carefully delineating when opinion entered, leaving personal evaluation out of the report, or couching it in the most cautious terms.

More and more, reporters have come to believe that if the objective facts demonstrate, for example, that we live in a racist country, and that the United States is engaged in a senseless, savage, and illegal war in Southeast Asia, it is the reporter's responsibility to report these facts and state candidly the conclusions drawn from them; it is the newspapers' responsibility to print them, and the networks' responsibility to broadcast and televise them. It is *not* the reporters' responsibility to misrepresent the facts, that is, to "balance" the news with "good" and "bad," so that the facts—the truth—will not appear so condemning.

But there are formidable obstacles to this practice, as Steve Knoll noted in *Variety* (December 31, 1969). His reference was to TV newsmen, but it applies equally to the media in general:

As newsmen, it is their traditional role to view the words and actions of government officials with a healthy skepticism, and to act as "watchdog" in behalf of the public interest. Yet they serve broadcast stations and networks that function primarily as purveyors of entertainment rather than as news media, and they are part of large and diversified corporations, many of them major defense contractors. In short, they operate in an environment where the fruits of any tough investigative reporting may well run counter to the interest of their employers' employers.

Agnew seemed to decry the power of the networks, but his principal target was the alleged power of the newsmen. His concern was not so much to diversify corporate control of the airwaves as to present news in a way more favorable to the Administration position. If this could be accomplished via corporate control, the Vice President would probably have no objection at all.

Nor would Attorney General Mitchell—and that is at the core of the subpoena controversy. For years the government has asked for, and been given, material by newspapers and radio-television networks on the basis of what might be called negotiated subpoenas—that is, subpoenas whose scope has been agreed upon by consultation in advance.

The demand for material periodically produced some grumbling but little publicity until late in January 1970, when CBS-TV was served with a subpoena to produce everything in CBS's possession involved in the shooting of a film about the Black Panthers—memos, notes, telephone calls, tapes and out-takes (tapes not edited or televised). It became known at the same time that three months earlier subpoenas had been served on four Chicago newspapers, and on *Time, Life, Newsweek,* and NBC News for unedited film, photographs, files, and even notebooks of reporters who had covered the Weathermen's "four days of rage" in Chicago in October 1969. *Time* and *Life* turned over their files, NBC negotiated with the Justice Department over the "mechanics" of the transmission. *Newsweek* deleted names before submitting its files, and CBS, after some vacillation, said it would seek to narrow the scope of its subpoena.

For working newspapermen and women, privacy and confidence are essential conditions in dealing with news sources. No source will continue to supply information if it knows that its origin will be revealed by the reporter, or if its information will be made available in court actions which may eventually involve the source. No federal law protects this special relationship between reporter and informant, but this state of confidence has long been given the status that derives from long practice. Fourteen states have laws which protect the rights of reporters not to divulge their news sources, and in March 1970 bills were introduced in the House and the Senate (the Newsmen's Privilege Act of 1970) to protect the working press from forced disclosure of confidential information.

There was widespread criticism of the Justice Department's actions, which was duly noted by Attorney General Mitchell. He responded in what has become standard operating procedure for the Nixon Administration: advance two brash steps, and retreat one step—so you're still ahead. On February 4, the day the *New York Times* published a strongly worded editorial in defense of the "unfettered flow of information to the public," Mitchell issued an "apology" which was less an apology than a justification. He regretted the furor which he attributed to a departure from the long-standing practice of "negotiations," and shrewdly listed a series of instances in which the media had cooperated fully with the government's requests. He did understand, Mitchell said, "the peculiar problems" the subpoenas raise for the press, and he would meet with media executives to reassure them in relation to these peculiarities.

A quiet corporate pilgrimage to Washington began. Julian Goodman, president of NBC, indicated that government "restraint" would solve the whole problem. He did not regard a common corporate strategy against the subpoenas as "practical," he said, because of the highly competitive nature of the communications industry. This was a clear signal to Mitchell that a united front of opposition would not be formed—not between newspapers and the networks (natural enemies in the war for the dollar), and not even among the networks themselves.

In August 1970, Attorney General Mitchell, after taking many soundings in the communications media, issued a set of "guidelines" for subpoenas which seemed, as the *New York Times* expressed it, to "reflect a welcome, if belated, recognition of the dangers inherent in any governmental intrusion on the news-gathering process." In fact, the new guidelines were hardly different from the practice prevailing before the rash of subpoenas several months earlier.

Mitchell selected the forum to announce his

guidelines carefully—the House of Delegates of the American Bar Association, meeting in St. Louis. He asked the lawyers to conduct a major study concerning the conflict between the government's search for evidence in criminal cases, and the contention of the working press that their sources of information would vanish if they were revealed publicly. Then he listed the new rules:

1. Recognizing that subpoenas may limit the freedom of the press, the Justice Department must weigh carefully this factor against the public interest.

2. The required information should be obtained wherever possible from other sources, and requests to the press made only as a last resort.

3. Before a subpoena is issued, the government should negotiate with the media to limit the subpoena.

4. Each subpoena must be authorized by the Attorney General himself.

5. Requests for authorization must demonstrate that the information is essential and unobtainable from other sources. In normal cases, subpoenas will be limited to verification of published or broadcast information. But they may be extended into the area of unpublished and unbroadcast material. Here "great caution" should be used.

The clue to Mitchell's general attitude came in the following section of his speech:

We will not permit an innocent man to be convicted or a guilty man to be freed because we decline to subpoena a newsman who has information vital to the case. And we may be on the threshold of a much broader controversy because we are now heading for a number of legal confrontations which could seriously mutate fundamental relationships among the government, the bar, and the courts.

The guidelines were vague enough and the At

torney General's power great enough to permit many confrontations. As for the request to his subordinates for "great caution," the temperate language hardly accorded with the character of the man himself. There was no doubt in Mitchell's mind, nor in the minds of the prospective recipients of the subpoenas, that the confrontations would come in the areas of the black freedom movement, the anti-war movement, and the university protest against war and racism.

Just five weeks after his speech to the bar association, and unencumbered by a prepared text, Mitchell's own caution was nowhere in evidence. In a "candid and convivial mood," according to a United Press International dispatch in the *Boston Globe* of September 19, 1970, he was interviewed by a woman reporter for *Women's Wear Daily* at a cocktail buffet at the Women's National Press Club in Washington. He characterized student and faculty dissidents as "these stupid bastards who are ruining our educational institutions" and declared that "this country is going so far right you are not even going to recognize it."

The *New York Times,* which had commented editorially and favorably on Mitchell's ABA speech, had no editorial comment on this convivial warning. The fact that the remarks may have been lubricated by several martinis made them perhaps more than less significant. But the communications industry chose not to notice.

It fell to a member of government to seek to stiffen the flaccid resolve of the industry executives. In a speech before a meeting of Harvard's Nieman Fellows (alumni of the Nieman program under which newspaper men and women spend a year of specialized study at Harvard), Nicholas

Johnson, gadfly FCC commissioner, declared that the freedom and the integrity of the press were in danger. He said:

It is shocking and saddening that the establishment press is so willing to acquiesce. The media have vast financial and legal resources at their command. The country could only benefit if they were to resist government encroachments upon their independence and defend in court their absolute First Amendment right to refuse such subpoenas.

Johnson declared that at the same time it was attacking TV-radio presentation of the news, the Administration was charting policies to protect the economic interests of the networks. Whether or not there was an actual deal, he said, "the results are very much the same as if there were a government-media agreement that the media will take care of the Administration's image if the government will take care of the media's balance sheets."

7

Preserve and protect

SUPPORTING JOHNSON'S estimate of the "sweet-heart" setup between the broadcasters and government, a deluge of bills has flooded Congress in the last year—without a sign of protest from the Administration—to protect the present holders of television channel franchises from challenge by groups that seek to obtain these franchises. The channels, of course, belong to the public, and are leased for three-year periods by license from the FCC. If a

challenger can prove that a present franchise holder
has not operated the channel in the public interest,
and that the challenger is equipped and willing to do
so, under the Communications Act of 1934, he may
be granted the franchise.

Until recently, however, the FCC has been noto-
riously protective of present license holders. It was
not until 1969 that the FCC vacated the license of a
channel held by the *Boston Herald-Traveler* and
awarded the channel occupied by WHDH-TV to a
group called Boston Broadcasters. Even then, four
commissioners did not vote, and the license was
vacated by a 2-1 decision. Under the prodding of
Commissioner Johnson and Kenneth Cox, an able
and fair-minded member of the FCC whose term
expired in 1970, and in whose place Nixon named
Leonard Unger, an attorney and long-time Nixon
campaign aide, the FCC had been applying the law
with greater vigor. But with Cox gone and Dean
Burch, a Goldwater campaign manager, as the
Nixon-appointed chairman of the FCC, it was expected that, in Burch's words, the FCC would
"level off."

An even graver danger than FCC vacillation was
an amendment to the Communications Act proposed by Senator John O. Pastore (Democrat of
Rhode Island). A zealous guardian of the morals of
the public against the alleged sinfulness of television programming, Pastore's economic morality
was nowhere in evidence in his amendment which
in effect would render impossible any real challenge
to the present channel holders. Under his proposal,
according to Jack Gould, television critic of the
New York Times, no competing application for an
existing channel could be entertained by the FCC
until the commission itself had first determined that
the present holder had not lived up to his respon-

sibilities. "If the wording of the amendment means what it says," Gould wrote, "the FCC would be required to rely primarily, if not wholly, on the representations of the license-holders."

The great value of a broadcast property (Gould estimated it at 90 per cent) rests in the occupancy of a channel, and the effect of the Pastore amendment would be to freeze the status quo even more rigidly than it is at present. The reluctance of the broadcast industry to lock horns with the government on issues raised by Agnew and Mitchell, or to look to Congress for relief from Administration pressure, would seem to support Commissioner Johnson's assertion that if an actual deal between government and the broadcast industry does not exist, there is at least an unspoken agreement. Nor does the fact that Pastore is a Democrat make any difference. When the corporate interest is at stake, party lines vanish in the rainbow at whose end lies the pot of gold.

A devastating indictment of the failure of the broadcast industry to live up to its responsibilities under the Communications Act, and its endless pursuit of profit, was presented in November 1969 in a report by the Alfred I. Du Pont Awards Foundation and Columbia University. Based on a year-long study, it concluded that most broadcasting "is a hideous waste of one of the nation's most important resources . . . the citizens' time and attention." What at best is "an incomparable means of communication, education, and inspiration, has become, more often than not, an insidious devourer, sapping the nation's energies and perforating its values."

The "real cause of the crisis in broadcasting," the report said, lies in what "a theologian would call greed," and what the industry calls "making a fair return on our investment." In language that seemed to spring more from Marx than Du Pont in its petition against private ownership of the broadcast industry (although it did not raise the question of broadcasting under public ownership), the report said:

> In what other business can a moderately astute operator hope to realize 100 per cent a year on the tangible assets, or lay out $150 for a franchise that in a few years' time he can peddle for $50 million—should he be so foolish as to want to sell? The most fantastic rewards associated with broadcasting in many instances grow from enterprises that do as little for their fellow countrymen as they legally can.

The findings of the Du Pont-Columbia report were gleefully recorded in *Editor & Publisher,* the spokesman for the newspaper industry, which never overlooks an opportunity to present the broadcasting industry in as poor a light as possible. But *Editor & Publisher* just as vigorously supported a piece of legislation concerning the newspaper industry which is as monstrous in its effect on the public interest as the Pastore amendment. This is the Newspaper Preservation Act, known before the Madison Avenue mechanics tampered with it, as the Failing Newspaper Act.

On July 24, 1970, President Nixon signed the legislation into law in a silent ceremony that went almost as unpublicized as the entire three-year campaign by the publishers to get the law enacted. In fact, there was not even an announcement of the signing until four days after the event.

Both the Failing Newspaper Act and the Newspaper Preservation Act which succeeded it (after the former had been talked to death in the House) were aimed at preserving arrangements then existing for 48 newspapers in 24 cities. Under these arrangements, newspapers in these cities shared printing facilities and advertising and subscription revenues, plus other production and business facilities, while maintaining separate editorial and news departments and policies.

A suit was brought to the Supreme Court under the anti-trust laws to end such an arrangement in Tucson, Arizona, between the *Star* and the *Citizen.* In March 1969 the court ruled that the arrangement did indeed violate the anti-trust laws against price-fixing, profit-pooling, and illegal market control. Following the decision, the newspaper industry went all out to force through a law which would in effect overturn the Supreme Court decision.

Rarely in modern history have publishers engaged in such active and intense lobbying on Capitol Hill. From Nashville came John Siegenthaler of the *Tennesseean;* from Honolulu, George Chaplin, editor of the *Advertiser;* from San Francisco, Charles Thierot, publisher of the *Chronicle*—in addition to executives of the Hearst, Scripps-Howard, and Ridder chains.

And rarely in modern history has a story of such significance been so completely blanked out in the press. Although there were more than two million words of testimony before the Senate Anti-Trust and Monopoly subcommittee, and exhibits filling 3,462 pages in seven volumes, some newspapers (including the two Tuscon newspapers) carried not a line on the hearings. Others published inadequate summaries, and almost none carried any editorials, either for or against. Even the *New York Times,* which sent an attorney to testify against the measure, published no editorial until January 31, 1970, eleven days after the Senate had passed the measure. It would have been impossible for even the most intelligent newspaper reader to have been able to determine the wisdom of the bill.

The bill was endorsed by a remarkably high percentage of members of both houses of Congress (33 Senators and 100 members of the House), including so-called liberals from states in which newspapers had big stakes in the bill. It was no surprise, then, when the bill was passed in the Senate on January 20, 1970, by a vote of 64 to 13, and in the House on July 8, by a vote of 292 to 87. When it came out of a House-Senate conference for a final Senate vote on July 15, there was only one recorded dissenting vote.

Despite the contention of the American Newspaper Publishers Association, and other proponents of the legislation, there was nothing in the Supreme Court decision forbidding joint plant operation and cost-sharing. The intent of the decision was to forestall monopoly practice which would make it impossible for competing newspapers to survive, and for new publications to undertake publication. The new law, while giving lip service to the idea of competition and independent editorial voices, almost guarantees that there will be no competition and little diversity of opinion.

A provision of the law says that one newspaper in any combination must demonstrate that it may be failing. But during the hearings not one newspaper involved in the 24 cities presented supportive evidence to this effect. Nor were the committee members, with the exception of Senator Philip Hart, (Democrat of Michigan), the chairman, very much interested in statistics. Thus, under the act, newspapers which are parties to joint agreements are absolved from liability in anti-trust suits. No other industry has this exemption. The law also requires that any future arrangement must have the approval of the Attorney General. With this condition, it is most unlikely that a combination seeking this approval will take editorial positions opposed to those of an Administration in which the Attorney General is perhaps the second most powerful figure, and a man of ruthless vindictiveness in addition.

Some years ago, when Lord Thomson acquired the rights to television in Scotland, he said he had at that moment been given "a license to print money." If the money tree thrives in Scotland, it is a miracle-growth plant in the United States. But Thomson's maxim does not apply to television alone: because of their 30 per cent interest in television stations, newspaper publishers get 34 per cent of all television revenue in the United States.

The newspaper lobbyists on Capitol Hill of course were aware of this, just as they knew also about the glowing report on the state of the newspaper industry published by *Forbes* magazine on October 1, 1969, at the peak of the crocodile-tear campaign about failing newspapers.

There are of course ailing newspapers, said *Forbes*, and there are even failing newspapers. But "despite the prophets of the electronic age, this does not prove that newspapers are a dying industry but that sudden death is a fact of life in the United States economy." In fact, said *Forbes*, newspapers have since 1945 "been remarkably stable." It concluded:

> On the whole, the newspaper industry has never been healthier, not even in the heyday of Joseph Pulitzer and William Randolph Hearst. Advertising revenues and circulation are increasing. Net income in recent years has represented a far greater return on revenues than those in other manufacturing industries. . . . Its a pretty lively corpse.

It is not many a corpse that can add another privilege such as the Newspaper Preservation Act to the number of privileges it already possesses.

One such privilege has traditionally been immune from criticism. As Arthur Rowse, a sound and vigorous critic of the press, wrote in *The Nation* on June 30, 1969, in an article on the Senate hearings concerning the Newspaper Preservation Act:

> The press has gained a reputation for prying secrets out of nearly every corner of life; and selling news to all who are willing to pay for it. But, as the Senate hearings have shown once again, the watchdog that watches everyone else is reluctant to tell secrets about itself. Apparently not even the power of Congress can expose the full story or slow the quest for still more privileges for the press.

For the word "press," read "publishers." Privileges for the working press were being diminished, as was being demonstrated in an action brought by Attorney General Mitchell against a reporter for the *New York Times*.

8

The black presence

IN THE 1969-1970 subpoena controversy, the most significant case was that of Earl Caldwell, a reporter for the *New York Times* assigned to the newspaper's San Francisco bureau. The case involved more than a reporter's right to keep his sources confidential. In the last analysis, it involved accurate and meaningful coverage of the black communities of America, both in the interest of fairness to black Americans, and to the education of white Americans as to their own responsibility for the conditions under which black America lives.

This fight for fairness is not a new one. Although it came to a climax in the 1960's, it reaches back 143 years to the founding of the first black paper in America. A brief background survey leading to the present situation can be informative.

One day in 1827, the Reverend Samuel Cornish and John B. Russworm, two black activists of the time, visited the editor of the *New York Sun*[3] to ask him to publish a story about a black organization of which they were members. The editor is reported to have told them: "The *Sun* shines bright for all white men, but never for the black man." The visitors walked out and undertook to found their own paper, named *Freedom's Journal.* It was the first of at least 24 black papers published before the Civil War. None of them lived long. The most effective of the group was Frederick Douglass's *North Star,* founded in Rochester, New York, in 1847. Its name was changed in 1850 to *Frederick Douglass's Paper,* and it survived until 1860.

In the last two decades of the 19th century and the first two of the 20th century, several influential papers were founded. Among them were the *New York Globe* (which later became the *Age*) in 1887; the *Washington Bee* (1882) guided throughout its 40-year life by William Calvin Chase, a gifted and courageous lawyer; the *Journal and Guide* of Norfolk, Virginia (1901), the *Chicago Defender* (1905), and the *Pittsburgh Courier* (1910).

The post-Civil War black press was vigorous in exposing the plight of the Freedmen. After the rise of the Ku Klux Klan and the spread of lynchings in the South, the *Chicago Defender,* during World War I, was credited with spurring the migration of black people to the North.

The number of black publications rose to about 150 in the 1940's, largely because of their leadership in the crusade for equality for the great number of black soldiers in the World War II army, and the growth in employment of black people in defense industries. In 1941 came the first great March on Washington, almost entirely ignored in the white press, which resulted in the first Executive Order, from President Franklin D. Roosevelt, for federal fair employment practices.

Total circulation of the black press in 1945 was placed at about 1.6 million. The big three were the *Pittsburgh Courier* (257,000), the *Chicago Defender* (202,000), and the *Baltimore Afro-American* (137,000). Gunnar Myrdal in his *An American Dilemma,* published that year, said: "The Negro press . . . is rightly characterized as the greatest single power in the Negro race."

Today there are more than 250 black publications with a circulation of over 2 million. There are, however, only two dailies (the *Chicago Defender,* with 33,000 readers, and the *Atlanta Daily World,* with 25,000). Only the *Afro-American* among the earlier leaders has maintained its former circulation. The new leaders, accounting for the entire circulation gain, are *Muhammad Speaks* (400,000), published by the Muslim movement, but with articles of broad interest, and the *Black Panther* (110,000). These figures in themselves bespeak the changing attitudes in the black communities and a militant orientation away from the general-circulation black press.

There are many reasons for the decline. Among them are the inroads of television and black radio. Inner-city blacks are "audio-oriented."[4] A Chicago black newspaper editor has said: "The four black-oriented radio stations here reach more listeners in an hour than the black newspaper has readers in a month."

More significant, however, is the fact that black newspapers have either not been able or willing to keep up with the rapidly changing moods of greater militancy and declining patience of the black communities. They are more parochial than their nationally-circulated forebears, and they emphasize social news for the black middle class and sensational news for the casual reader. More and more, the black reader looks to the larger white paper in his community for news about blacks, even though he may regard much of this news with skepticism.

Here we come to the link between the Caldwell subpoena and the black readership.

The 1960's saw a new phenomenon in the general white press: the rise of the black journalist. Until then, most big newspapers had one token black editorial person, or at best two or three. Some had none at all. The efforts of the American Newspaper Guild to break down the race barriers in its formative years in the 1930's were unavailing. At the *New York Times,* for example, the number of black maintenance workers (under Guild jurisdiction) were in the hundreds. There were one or two blacks in editorial positions.

Two factors were basically responsible for the change: (1) the opening market for goods in the black communities which were vocally resentful of lily-white packaging, including news products; (2) the influence of the black freedom movement which had helped to stir black people to the point where it had become impossible for white reporters to gather the news in a largely hostile black community. These two elements combined to make it necessary, both for economic and for socio-political reasons, to have a larger black presence, both in advertising and in the news columns, in the white press—and on white television. If the black community was "audio-oriented," it also had eyes to see.

A new kind of spark was ignited on February 2, 1970, when Caldwell was served with a new kind of subpoena—directed at him and not the *New York Times*—ordering him to testify before a federal grand jury about the Black Panthers. Specifically he was ordered to bring tape recordings and notes of interviews with Panther leaders David Hilliard and Raymond Masai Hewitt.

Caldwell declared that he would not appear. The *Times* assigned lawyers and company officials to advise him, and asserted it would use "all its resources to make sure that no judicial action violates the constitutional guarantees of a free press." But it did not say it would instruct Caldwell not to appear.

The subpoena aroused black journalists from coast to coast. Black reporters for the newspapers and the networks hold a special place in the black community. For generations the needs and the hopes of the black community were non-news for the communications media. But the pressure of events and the ever-increasing focus on racial affairs forced the white media to take steps to improve its coverage.

For the first time, beginning in the middle 1960's, news of black people in the general press took on a new dimension—a human one. While there were conflicts among black journalists themselves about the balance of professionalism and politics, there was no conflict about color and commitment. This was reflected in the almost universal confidence the black community gave to black journalists. And it is precisely this link of commitment and confidence that the Justice Department was seeking to break by the subpoena to Caldwell.

The government's intent was apparent to the nation's black journalists and they reacted immediately. A statement signed by 70 leading black writers appeared as a full-page advertisement in the black press. It emphasized that Caldwell had been served as an individual, that the government felt that as a black man he had special access to information in the black community. The statement declared:

> Thus the role of every black news man and woman has been put into question—Are we government agents? Will we reveal confidential sources if subpoenaed? Can our employers turn over our files, notes, or tapes if we object? We do not intend to be used as spies, informers, or undercover agents by anybody—period! We will protect our confidential sources, using every means at our disposal. . . . We are black journalists attempting to interpret, with as great understanding and truth as is possible, the nation's social revolutions.

To underscore the individual nature of his subpoena, Caldwell engaged his own lawyer, Anthony Amsterdam, a professor at Stanford University Law School. After legal moves both by the *Times* and by Caldwell to quash the subpoena, Caldwell was served again in mid-March 1970. This time he was not required to bring his notes and tapes, but he was ordered to testify about his confidential sources. On April 3, Federal District Court Judge Alfonso C. Zirpoli in San Francisco ruled that Caldwell would have to appear before a grand jury, but that he could not be compelled to disclose confidential information unless there was a "compelling national interest that cannot be served by alternate means."

The *Times* and many legal authorities regarded the Zirpoli ruling as a "landmark decision," and it was indeed the first time that any court had limited the government in this manner. But Caldwell, while willing to authenticate his published story in open court, refused to become a party to secret testimony before a grand jury on the ground that it would make him appear as an investigative arm of government. The *Times,* clearly disappointed, did not associate itself with Caldwell's appeal against the Zirpoli ruling. The appeal was rejected, and a new subpoena was issued for Caldwell to appear before a new grand jury.

Once again the *Times* came back into the picture (since the process started all over again) and associated itself with Caldwell's effort to quash the new subpoena. The move failed, and Caldwell on June 5 was found in contempt of court. Again he appealed and, since the only possible ruling on the appeal was whether Caldwell should be forced to appear, the *Times* again joined in, noting that the conditions set by Judge Zirpoli would prevail and could be cited as precedent if other staff reporters were subpoenaed.

On November 17, 1970, in a decision of the utmost significance, the federal Ninth Circuit Court of Appeals supported Caldwell's refusal to appear before the grand jury, and ruled that the government must show a pressing need for evidence before ordering a journalist to testify in secret. Demonstrating an unusual sensitivity about the relationship of black militant groups to news reporters (the decision even referred to "the 'Establishment' press"), the court said:

"The very concept of a free press requires that the news media be accorded a measure of autonomy; that they should be free to pursue their own investigation to their own ends without fear of governmental interference, and that they should be able to protect their investigative processes."

Turning reporters into "investigative agents of the government," the decision said, "cannot be justified in the public interest."

For Caldwell, and for other black news men and women, there are other problems evolving from their work on white newspapers, and the keenness with which they are aware of these problems accounts for the formation of all-black associations within the media. One is Black Perspective, a group with representatives in New York, Washington, and other Eastern cities, which seeks not only to guarantee fairness for black personnel in the media, but ways and means of ensuring fairness in the coverage of the black community.

On the West Coast, a group called the Black Journalists in the Bay Area publishes a monthly tabloid, *Ball & Chain,* devoted to the problems of blacks in the media. The Caldwell case took up an entire recent issue. In its second issue, *Ball & Chain* published an interview with Hoyt Fuller, managing editor of the magazine *Black World* (formerly the *Negro Digest*) about the black press.

Fuller noted the cleavage between the black militants and the black press which, he said, "represents essentially the interests of the black bourgeoisie." There are both economic and political reasons why the brightest of the young black journalists are heading for the white press or into public relations, he said. The black press cannot pay the young journalists what they should be getting (only 10 of 156 black newspapers are unionized), and the owners regard the young journalists as a threat to their own position of racial moderation.

The problem of the black press is compounded by the infinitely greater resources of the white press now available to black journalists working there.

Hoyt did not regard the increased coverage of the black community as a "fad that is going to pass." He said:

I don't think that the white press is going to return to its prior position of ignoring the black community. But I do think the black community is turning inward and is no longer interested in having its activities interpreted for it by the white press. It is no longer interested in having anything interpreted for it by the white press, and that is why blacks will turn more and more toward their own newspapers. Its our own realization, finally, of who the enemy is and where he is, and the futility of continually, generation after generation, butting your head against the wall expecting white people in general, and the white press in particular, to be fair and honest and to deal with black people from a black perspective. This is absolutely impossible, and black people are becoming more and more aware of that. The black press must preform its job, and I put the responsibility on the black press to be not only relevant but first rate in all that it does.

While *Muhammad Speaks* and the *Black Panther* do not fulfill the qualifications of journalistic excellence that Hoyt sets forth, it is clear that their large circulation, particularly among black people who are neither Muslims nor Panthers, testifies to the accuracy of Hoyt's sense of new directions in the black community. If and when the young black journalists of the white press, with their accrued experience and knowledge of the operations of the white power structure—of which the white press is a potent arm—accept Hoyt's challenge, a new black press could emerge that does meet his specifications. It would be not only relevant and first rate, but it could be a unifying and activating force of tremendous power in the black community.

9

The radical press

IT MAY be difficult for Americans in the 1970's to believe, but at one point in its 27-year career an American socialist publication was the most widely read newspaper in the country. It was the weekly *Appeal to Reason,* the most successful and effective radical publication ever published in the United States, which once reached a circulation of over a million readers. At the height of its influence, it maintained a circulation of 400,000 for several years. One reason was Eugene Victor Debs.

The *Appeal* was founded in 1895 by Julius Wayland, an Indiana Republican who had grown wealthy as a printer and real estate man, and then turned to the socialism of Edward Bellamy (*Looking Backward*). Historian Ray Ginger relates [5] that the William Jennings Bryan "craze" of 1896, which demolished the populist movement in the Democratic Party, almost extinguished the *Appeal* at its start. After a temporary suspension, Wayland made a fresh start at Girard, Kansas, and by 1899 had 100,000 readers.

Debs joined Big Bill Haywood and other labor leaders in founding the Industrial Workers of the World in 1905. In December of that year, Frank Steunenberg, governor of Idaho, was killed by a bomb and a miner was arrested on suspicion. He gave the Pinkertons (industrial police) a "confession" that he had been hired by Haywood, Charles

Moyer, and George Pettibone—leaders of the Western Federation of Miners—to kill the governor because Steunenberg had called the militia to break the strike of the Coeur d'Alene miners in 1899.

Debs, recalling the Chicago Haymarket frameup of a decade earlier, wrote a protest and sent it to the *Appeal*. It was so inflamatory that the *Appeal's* editor hesitated to print it. Wayland looked it over and said: "The only question I want you to settle in your mind before acting is: will it work to the best interests of socialism?"

The article ran under the heading: "AROUSE, YE SLAVES!" It warned the authorities that "if they attempt to murder Moyer, Haywood, and their brothers, a million revolutionists at least will meet them with guns."

From then on, Debs wrote weekly in the *Appeal* on the case, and it was at this time that the *Appeal* passed the million mark. One single issue, Ginger wrote, required "ten barrels of ink, six carloads of newsprint, three thousand mailbags, and ten United States Mail cars." The prosecution of the IWW leaders dragged on through 1906 and into 1907, and by the time the trial opened in May 1907, Debs had pricked President Theodore Roosevelt into comment: he judged Debs guilty along with Haywood and Moyer.

In Boise, Idaho, the jury disagreed with the President, and all were acquitted. But the *Appeal* then became subject to vindictive reprisal. Debs and editor Fred Warren were indicted on charges of sending "scurrilous, defamatory, and threatening material" through the mails. Warren was tried first in 1909, convicted, sentenced to six months in jail, and fined $10,000. An appeal was taken and Debs and Warren converted the campaign into a subscription-building contest. When they first started on tour, circulation stood at 369,000. Before the year was over, it had reached 500,000.

Warren's conviction was upheld, and another national campaign was undertaken. President Taft, seeking to reduce the feverish pitch, struck out the six-month sentence, reduced the fine to $100 and sent Warren a pardon. Warren looked the pardon over and sent it back with a demand for a union label. He said he would pay the fine in *Appeal* subscription cards. Taft, a more cagey politician than he is often credited with being, bowed out of the affair, and Warren never paid the fine.

The *Appeal,* with Debs as a contributing editor, went on to fight the frameup in 1910 of the McNamara brothers in the dynamiting of the *Los Angeles Times* building in which 21 were killed. Debs charged that the owners of the *Times* were themselves guilty. The *Appeal* also sparked the 1912 presidential campaign in which Debs got 900,000 votes on the Socialist ticket. The Republican Taft Administration, retiring for the victorious Democrat, Woodrow Wilson, took a parting shot at the *Appeal.* A new set of indictments was obtained against Debs, Warren, and publisher Wayland growing out of a series of muckraking articles on the federal penitentiary at Leavenworth, Kansas. They were never presented, but as a new frameup was being prepared against Wayland, then 58, he went home one night, considered his situation, and blew his brains out. In a much-read copy of Bellamy's *Looking Backward,* Wayland had stuck a note which read: "The struggle under the capitalist system isn't worth the effort. Let it pass."

Debs, heartbroken over Wayland's suicide, resigned his editorship on the *Appeal.* A colleague wired Wayland's son: "We shed no tears of grief.

Grief is for the naked lives of those who have made the world no better."

The weekly continued publication, with one World War I interruption, and folded finally in 1922. But until its publisher was hounded to his death, the *Appeal to Reason* gave the populists, socialists, and progressives of America just about the greatest run anybody ever got for his money in the press.

The *Appeal* was the most exciting and widely read radical paper of the time, but the various factions of the Socialist Party, with its membership at about 100,000 in 1912, published more than 300 papers and periodicals, among them five English-language and eight foreign-language dailes. The Espionage Act of 1917, aimed at anti-war newspapers, successfully hampered the distribution of the Socialist press by voiding their mailing rights. Among the victims were Victor Berger's *Milwaukee Leader* and the *New York Call,* which was still fighting in 1923 for its mailing privileges. It was turned down in the Supreme Court and, after a brief flurry under the editorship of Norman Thomas, died that same year.

In the late 1920's and the depression years of the 1930's, radical journalism never achieved a standing commensurate with the organizing opportunities of the time. The Socialist Party was in disarray and, at the height of the depression in 1936, was split in two. Some Socialist-oriented weeklies in the 1930's did have a brisk period of popularity—Oscar Ameringer's *American Guardian,* for example, reached a circulation of 40,000, largely because of the sharp and witty personal style of the editor—but they soon faded.

In his book *Lords of the Press* (Julian Messner, 1938), George Seldes noted that at the time there were 570 labor publications in the United States with a circulation of close to nine million. But they were not read with great interest by the majority of working people, nor did they have great influence.

In general, the quality of trade union papers has not been high. Many have been puff sheets for union leaders; others have been poorly edited and presented. Professional journalists were not easily attracted to the labor field. Sporadic efforts to publish daily labor newspapers rarely persevered, and most of the weeklies were dull.

There have been exceptions, however. The *Seattle Daily Call,* which was followed by the *Seattle Union Record,* grew out of the great Seattle general strike of 1919, and gave a start in journalism to such distinguished radicals as Harvey O'Connor and Anna Louise Strong.

The *CIO News* under the editorship of Len DeCaux served with distinction during the rise of industrial unionism. The *People's Press,* founded in the early 1930's, achieved a circulation of about 250,000. It was an independent weekly of general interest, but it was supported by the unions and published special regional editions in time of strike crises. The weekly *Labor,* founded at the end of World War I, reached a circulation of 500,000, but its editor Edward Keating failed to persuade Samuel Gompers, head of the AFL, to support the establishment of a chain of labor papers across the country.

This lack of interest was dismaying in view of the general press's unyielding hostility to labor's interests. In his book *The Press and Its Problems* (William C. Brown, 1964), Curtis D. MacDougall cited innumerable instances of suppression and distortion of news of labor during the 1930's and 1940's.

The most effective radical publication of the depression years was the *Daily Worker,* which espoused the views of the Communist Party of the United States. It helped spark the organizing of the unemployed, campaigned against racism, supported the hunger marches on Washington, and fought against the rise of fascism in Spain and Germany. It also took up the cause of industrial unionism, as against the craft unionism of the American Federation of Labor, which led to the founding of the CIO in 1935. In the 1930's, the membership of the Communist Party was at its peak—about 80,000— and the *Daily Worker* circulation stood at about 35,000. The week-end *Worker* reached 100,000.

Inevitably, the publication's fortunes rose and fell with that of the party, whose policies were strongly affected by the tides of international events. Committed as it was to the defense of the Soviet Union as the first—and then only—socialist government, the party was severly affected by the Soviet-German non-aggression treaty of 1939, and the opposition to it in the United States. Its popular support declined further in the early years of World War II, which it characterized as an "imperialist war," before the German attack on the Soviet Union in June 1941. In the years following World War II, financial problems, coupled with an inability to obtain the services of professionally competent journalists—many of them sympathetic but fearful of association—caused another decline in the fortunes of the *Daily Worker*. There was further attrition as the party and its leaders bore the main brunt of the Cold-War witch hunt of the late 1940's and early 1950's, when first the Truman Doctrine and then the McCarthy terror and the Korean War enveloped the country in a hysteria generated by the myth of the "international communist conspiracy."

In 1958, the *Daily Worker* was converted into the weekly *Worker,* then published for a time twice a week, and finally, in 1968, renamed the *Daily World,* which began publishing as a daily newspaper using photo composition and offset printing. Its circulation in 1970 was 24,000, an increase of 8,000 over the previous year.

Since World War II, a West Coast counterpart of the East Coast Communist press was published in San Francisco as the *People's World,* which in turn was a successor to the *Western Worker.* It was for many years a daily but became a weekly in the late 1950's. It put greater stress on domestic coverage and at times evidenced a more flexible approach in its news stories, editorial comment and published correspondence from its readers.

The radical press of the post-World War II years reflected the polarization of political opinion in the radical movement in the United States and the defensive posture of radicals. They faced not only the frontal attacks by government, but also the hostility of so-called "democratic socialists" whose basic creed was not socialism but anti-communism, and the fear-ridden silence of the liberals longing for a return of the days of the Rooseveltian New Deal.

Among the other radical weeklies of continuing publication is the *Weekly People,* organ of the Socialist Labor Party, now in its 80th year of publication, with a circulation of 10,000. Like its party parent, the *Weekly People* is sober and purist in declaring itself to be the only true Marxist publication in the country, according to the teachings and interpretations of the party's most illustrious figure, Daniel DeLeon. It appears to have little influence on young radicals.

The *Militant,* the weekly newspaper of the Socialist Workers Party (Trotskyist), has continued publication, except for a two-year hiatus—1937-

38—since its founding in 1928. Its circulation in 1970 was 20,000. Unlike the *Weekly People,* the *Militant* is very much involved in the affairs of the radical movement, and publishes frequent analyses, many of them controversial, of the various trends within the movement.

A significant departure in American radical journalism, which might be classified as prematurely New Left, took place at the height of the Cold War. It was the appearance within a three-year period— late 1948 to 1952—of three independent publications, two of them weekly and one a monthly, most accurately described as non-communist leftist. Each evidenced dissatisfaction with what it regarded as the circumscribed publications of the existing parties of the organized Left, and sought to find a readership and sphere of influence beyond the organized left.

They were the *National Guardian,* founded in 1948 by Cedric Belfrage, John T. McManus, and the author of this book, with the subtitle "Independent Progressive Weekly," although its content and editorial positions could be more aptly described as radical; the *Monthly Review,* founded in 1949 by Leo Huberman and Paul M. Sweezy, as an independent socialist publication (and since it never sought to become a newspaper in any sense of the term, it is introduced here only because of the politically significant coincidence of its appearance); and *I. F. Stone's Weekly* (1952), based in Washington, which analyzed national and foreign policy from what is best described as a nonconformist socialist muckraking point of view.

The *National Guardian* reached a top circulation of 54,000 in 1950, when a combination of the Korean War and McCarthyism caused its reader ship to decline to 22,000. In the course of its career, it vigorously defended the rights of the Communist leaders indicted under the Smith Act, sparked a world-wide campaign in defense of Julius and Ethel Rosenberg, who were executed in 1953, took up the cause of independent political action on the Left as against support of the major political parties, and anticipated the rise of the black freedom movement and the New Left white radical movement. For its militancy, its founding editor Belfrage was forced to leave the United States (he was a British citizen) in 1953.

The *National Guardian* resisted internal dissension until the mid-1960's, when the stresses and strains of conflict within the radical movement in general became insurmountable. The founding management was succeeded in 1967 by a new group, and the name of the paper was changed to the *Guardian.* It has shifted its point of view according to the fortunes of dominant groups within the *New Left.*

In 1970, a dissident group broke away from the Guardian and founded a *Liberated Guardian.* Both continued publication, the *Guardian* as a "Marxist-Leninist" weekly, and the *Liberated Guardian* as a free-wheeling anarchistic publication of less regular appearance.

The most widely read of the independent publications and still showing a steady advance in 1970 is *I. F. Stone's Weekly,* with a circulation of 65,000, and a national readership that crosses the political lines in government, industry, and the professions. The basic reason for its success and esteem is the indefatigable research and acid comment by Stone on national and international affairs. The acquiescence of the vast majority of the Washington press corps to the policies of government has given Stone a remarkably clear field of operation.

However advanced these publications may have been, they confronted still another phenomenon in the 1960's. This was the so-called underground press.

Begun as a subjective protest against "the system," and advocating a life style of bizarre dress, drugs, and sexual freedom, the underground press in the last years of the 1960's had surfaced to become a political entity of considerable appeal, with a potential that caused concern in the established media.

In 1970, there were about 450 such newspapers, most of which had replaced scores of already defunct publications, and many of which had little hope for a long life-span. But others had been publishing successfully for years, and the total circulation for the underground press as a whole in mid-1970 was estimated at three million. Further, as disenchantment with the system grew, the anti-establishment press spread to colleges and high schools and to Army posts (at least 45 papers at this writing were being produced by servicemen).

The underground press appealed to an audience which has become persuaded that the regular press (this term is used instead of "commercial press" because many so-called underground papers have become highly commercial by means of advertising) is neither accurate, candid, no complete. It is staffed, with varying degrees of efficiency and experience, by young people who are willing to work for very little compensation, or none at all, simply as part of their life style—and who, because of their admirable lack of avarice, are too often exploited.

The development of offset printing methods has enabled low-cost publication, although distribution and regularity remain problems. The effectiveness of the underground press, and the alarm it has caused in the established institutions, are demonstrated by the withdrawal of large advertising by recording companies (mainly of rock music), as the producers of the dissenting newspapers have become aware that millionaire rock groups are not the most effective channel to revolution, and have begun to look elsewhere—particularly toward socialism—for political solutions.

In the usual pattern of affluent seduction, some early underground newspapers have become plump with advertising and correspondingly lean in their quest for social and political change. A few still adhere to the diminishing psychedelic approach, with its stress on drugs and withdrawal from society, but these publications are regarded by their comtemporaries with amused tolerance.

Attending the needs of the underground press and the college newspapers (which in many parts of the country have taken a leading part in the campus revolts) are press services operating in the manner of the conventional press services, although their content and financing are entirely unconventional. One is the Underground Press Service, a cooperative which permits members to reprint one another's articles. The other is Liberation News Service, which sells its output of news, photographs, and cartoons to about 200 newspapers and organizations—including the Library of Congress, CBS, *Life* magazine, the Soviet news agency Tass, and Peking's New China News Agency.

As has so often happened before with movements for change, the sharp-eyed and sharp-eared spokesman for established institutions of American society have adapted the superficial aspects of the life style of the "underground" to the profit motive. Thus several regular newspapers instituted a weekly "youth page" in which the language and feature material of the underground press were imitated. Advertisements for ladies fashions and for soft drinks, a survey reported, "have appeared in the total-impact style of overall design and dazzling color so familiar to the readers of underground newspapers."[6]

This practice has carried over into television advertising and programming, and into singing and musical commercials on radio, where the rock motif has been adopted by purveyors of deodorants, detergents, breakfast foods, and refrigerators. New magazines making their appearance in the last few years, as the mass circulation magazines with their wholesomely commercial approach have begun to fail, have sought their audiences among a free-swinging young readership. The approach has been financially successful, in some cases, but has missed the mark entirely in understanding what the young rebellion is all about—if it ever sought to understand.

Law enforcement agencies, however, and the dominating interests in cities where effective under-ground publications have appeared, are clear in their understanding of the best of the underground press and its purpose.

In San Diego, for example, where the two dailies are owned and operated by the ultra-conservative James S. Copley chain, the *Street Journal and San Diego Free Press* was harrased continually by city officials and the police. This newspaper, remarkably free of four-letter words, was willing even to criticize the "pretentious dialogue" of a film like *Easy Rider,* which has been canonized in much of the underground press, and as *Time* magazine put it, "manages to denounce pollution and corruption without invoking Mao Tse-tung." It suffered bullets through its windows, theft, smashed equipment, fire bombings, and repeated arrest on charges which were subsequently thrown out.

In Los Angeles, the editor of the *Los Angeles Free Press* and a reporter were convicted on a charge of receiving stolen goods—in this case, information. The *Free Press* in August 1969 published the names and addresses of secret narcotics agents, obtained from a photostat list received from a clerk at the Attorney General's Los Angeles office; and a report of an investigation of alleged criminal activities by police of the University of California. The conviction and fines, which have been appealed, could mean the end of the newspaper, currently with a circulation of 100,000 weekly.

Among other actions of deliberate persecution:

In Cambridge, street salesmen of Boston's *Avatar* achieved a total of 58 arrests for peddling allegedly obscene material before a judge ruled that the material was not obscene. By this time numerous newsstands had been frightened into refusing to carry the paper, and the circulation suffered a sharp decline.

In Montgomery County, Maryland, the editor of the *Washington Free Press* was sentenced to six months in prison for publishing an allegedly obscene cartoon of a judge.

In Chicago, the editor of *Seed* was arrested for publishing a Christmas collage of nudes, police, skulls, sexual acts, and lots more, in a pungent comment on American society.

In Madison, Wisconsin, the editor of the *Madison Kaleidoscope* was sentenced to six months for contempt when he refused to appear before a grand jury to disclose the source of a document published in the newspaper attributed to a group claiming responsibility for the bombing of the Army Mathematics Research Center on the University of Wisconsin campus. In handing down the sentence, the judge said the case was a clash between justice and the right of freedom of the press, and "something has to give." He concluded: "What has to give is the First Amendment privilege—in the interest of justice." The editor later agreed to testify.

The significance of the Madison case, as of all the others cited, is that the law enforcement agencies were at bottom seeking to halt not the spread of alleged obscenity, but criticism of American institutions. If obscenity actually was the target, there was another wide-open, if legally doubtful, area of activity: the openly pornographic newspapers on public sale in thousands of newsstands and shops across the country which have no relationship whatever to the underground press. Yet these publications, except in rare cases, have been allowed to publish and to be sold mainly because they have no controversial political comment, and because they are purchased not by young people but by middle-aged and elderly Americans. The youth rebellion has little need of pornographic material to stimulate a healthy sexual revolution.

The underground press, whenever it turns political, thus runs into established hostility. If it can surmount this opposition, it still must develop a greater maturity and a perspective which will help it point the way to an alternative society to the one it so validly rejects.

10

Cuba and Vietnam

DESPITE THE tenacity of the traditional radical press and the mushroom growth of the underground press, the combined effectiveness of this press is not great among the general public. This is one reason why there has not been greater open harassment of these publications—yet.

But it is appropriate at this point to ask why there is such vehemence and continuity in the attack against large sections of a communications industry which for the most part has served voluntarily as a virtual propaganda arm of government since the end of World War II. Documentation for this latter charge is not difficult: it is recorded in the pages of the press and in the broadcasts of television commentators who have become household idols placed in niches once reserved for film stars of the Hollywood days of glory. And it concerns itself largely with foreign policy.

Of the coverage of Cuba, for example, Herbert L. Matthews, a distinguished foreign correspondent and until his retirement in 1969 a member of the editorial board of the *New York Times,* said in 1961: "In all my 39 years on the *New York Times,* I have never seen a big story so misunderstood and so badly handled as the Cuban Revolution." That statement holds valid more than ten years after the revolution.

Matthews, it will be recalled, had that famous

interview with Fidel Castro in the Sierra Maestra mountains of Cuba on February 24, 1957, after Castro had been reported by the American communications media to be probably dead and the revolution smashed. The interview made Matthews "the most controversial figure to have come out of Cuba besides Fidel Castro," the *Christian Science Monitor* wrote. He was charged by both the government and many of his colleagues of the press, in effect, with ressurecting Castro from an American-made grave, and "losing Cuba for us," just as the American reporters who exposed the corruption and venality of the Chiang Kai-shek regime in China "lost China for us."

The role of the *Times* in the Bay of Pigs fiasco in 1961 and the missile crisis of 1962 has been documented with precision in an article in the *Columbia University Forum*[7] and by a managing editor of the *Times* itself.[8] In both instances, the *Times* had in its possession information which, if published, might have averted needless death and destruction in 1961, and the frightening confrontation between the United States and the Soviet Union in 1962.

On April 27, 1961, when *Times* executive editor Turner Catledge visited the White House with several other editors and publishers to discuss the coverage of the Bay of Pigs with President Kennedy, the President took Catledge aside and said: "If you had printed more about the operation you would have saved us from a colossal mistake." Of course, if the *Times* had "printed more," Kennedy would have been furious (he was, in any case, angry at the press after the fiasco). But in retrospect he was right: publication might have braked the military and diplomatic apparatus of state—however temporarily—as it moved ahead on its disaster course.

The fact is that the press, by refusing to become an automatic arm of foreign policy, can help prevent disaster. In the missile crisis, both the *Times* and the *Washington Post* knew what the President and the Defense Department were planning but, at Kennedy's request, withheld the information despite the near-panic that set in across the nation because of fear of atomic war. The decision that confronted the press was made clear in an article by Max Frankel of the *New York Times* Washington staff (he is now chief of bureau) on October 23, 1962. Noting the various reasons why the secrecy was not broken by the newspapers which were aware of what was going on, Frankel wrote:

> The basic reason was the fear that the Soviet Union, if it knew the blockade plans in advance, would make some move to undercut the President's course. For example, one such move might have been a resolution in the United Nations.

In other words, the newspapers, with the *New York Times* setting the example, kept the secret lest the United States be forced to adhere to the United Nations Charter and not take unilateral action with impunity. The conclusion one is forced to make is that the press refused to exercise its responsibility to restrain a reckless government from taking illegal action which might have brought on World War III.

The role of the communications media on Vietnam, going back to the first Kennedy buildup with American "advisers" in 1961, has been a contradictory one. Here again the inpact of television has been the most striking aspect of the coverage of the war.

From the early days of the regime of Ngo Dinh Diem, whom the government and the press sought to portray as "the Winston Churchill of Asia" (credit for the phrase goes to Lyndon B. Johnson, after a fact-finding trip as Vice President), there was a conflict between press and government, and among the press corps itself.

Top honors for candor and honesty must go to a group of newspaper correspondents who sought valiantly, and with some success, to expose the ugliness of the Diem regime and the callousness and stupidity of American officialdom in Saigon. Among them were Homer Bigart and David Halberstam of the *New York Times,* Malcolm Browne of the Associated Press, Charles Mohr of *Time* magazine, and Neil Sheehan of United Press International (Browne, Mohr, and Sheehan are all now with the *Times*); and several television newsmen—Morley Safer and John Laurence of CBS were outstanding—who risked their lives under fire of the enemy, and their reputations under fire of the government.

The reporting by these men was anathema to Washington, and in addition caused considerable uneasiness in the home offices of the newspapers and networks. *Time* magazine, for example, asked Mohr for a story on the press corps in Saigon, then discarded his article, and ordered an entirely different version written in New York which pictured the courageous journalists (as against the run-of-the-mill hacks) as a group of whimpering, neurotic, and prejudiced neophytes who never got out of the hotel bar. Mohr promptly quit *Time.*

Periodically, too, under pressure from the White House, or even without pressure, the publishers sent out a corrective corps of correspondents (the Hearst press, Scripps-Howard and the *New York Hearld Tribune* were regulars on this run) who could be counted on to send back glowing reports of progress—reports completely at variance with

those of the "young Turks" who, according to their
detractors, wanted to "lose Vietnam for us"—just
as China and Cuba were lost. The most venomous
of the journalistic critics of the journalists was
columnist Joseph Alsop, who conducted himself in
Vietnam like a general, and whose treatment by the
American high command was in accord with that
usually reserved for generals. His reports on such
occasions read like orders to the troops—and to the
Pentagon. The only problem was that they were just
as short-sighted and as arrogant as the Pentagon's
own reports.

Courageous as the small group of honest reporters were, they seemed at the time to be unable
to relate their findings to the underlying goals of
American foreign policy. The burden of their reports was that there was no possibility of pursuing
the war to a victorious end in collaboration with
Vietnamese governments like that of Diem, or with
the kind of myopic functionaries who served the
United States in Saigon. If these people could be
replaced, they maintained, then the war could be
pursued with renewed vigor and efficiency, and with
the possibility of military success.

These reporters despised the venal and corrupt
Vietnamese supported by the United States, and
admired the tenacity and bravery of the regime's
opponents. But none of them seemed then to understand that the main cause of the misery was trace-
able not to men like Diem, but to the American
presence in Vietnam and all of Southeast Asia.

Most of the reporters wrote books about their
experiences when they came back to the United
States after long tours of duty. And while their
straight reportage of what they had seen amounted
to a devastating indictment of American and Vietnamese officials, they never got down to an analysis

of American policy or, above all, of the aspirations of the people of Vietnam, north and south. These factors, after all, had brought the National Liberation Front of South Vietnam into being, and had inspired the people of North Vietnam to withstand the cruelest bombings and fight back with ever-increasing determination.

In the last few years, some of the reporters in this group have come to see the futility of the war and have spoken out against it. But it remains to be seen whether, when a similar crisis occurs again, they will hold fast to their new consciousness or revert, in the "national interest," to their support of a war policy.

As for the position of their employers, the *Boston Globe*, at the beginning of 1968, undertook a survey of editorial opinion among 39 major American newspapers, with a total circulation of 22 million, to determine their views on the war. The results showed that several newspapers in the previous months had become critical of the escalation of the war, and some had become "more hawkish." But not one newspaper advocated withdrawal of American troops from Vietnam, although millions of their readers in surveys, polls, letters, and demonstrations had expressed themselves in favor of withdrawal. It is more than likely that the result would have been the same if the survey had been extended to cover all 1,758 daily newspapers in the United States. Today, although a few newspapers, like the *Los Angeles Times* cited earlier, have advocated withdrawal over a period of time, still not one newspaper has called editorially for *immediate* withdrawal.

11

The dinner-table war

THE MOST cogent reason for immediate withdrawal from Vietnam is presented every evening on the television screen by American television from Indochina. This is how CBS's Morley Safer described television at war:[9]

This is television's first war. It is only in the past few years that the medium has become portable enough to go out on military operations. And this has raised some serious problems—problems, incidentally, which every network correspondent and cameraman in Vietnam is acutely aware of.

The camera can describe in excruciating, harrowing detail what war is all about. The cry of pain, the shattered face—it's all there on film, and out it goes to millions of American homes during the dinner hour. It is true that on its own every piece of war film takes on a certain anti-war character, simply because it does not glamorize or romanticize. . . .Television tells it that way. It also tells what happens to civilians who are caught in the middle of battle. It tells what happens to soldiers under stress of the unreal condition in which they live.

The unfavorable has always been reported along with the favorable—but television tells it with greater impact. When the U.S. blunders television leaves little doubt. So when a government official, either in Saigon or Washington, denies what television plainly reports and then attempts to give verisimilitude to his denial by damning the reporters—at best that is pure humbug.

A supreme example of humbuggery, with sinister

overtones, in which the government attacked not only reporters but a network itself, was given in the winter and spring of 1969-70. The antagonists were Clark Mollenhoff, a special assistant to the President whose duties were in effect to be house detective for the Administration, and CBS-TV. Mollenhoff for years had been an investigative reporter for the *Des Moines Register and Tribune,* a Cowles publication, and had earned a reputation as a righteous scourge of governmental bureaucrats. His approach has sometimes been described as a "Mollenhoff cocktail."

The affair had its origin in a CBS-TV broadcast from Vietnam on November 3, 1969, curiously enough the same day as Nixon's controversial report to the nation on Vietnam appealing to the "silent majority." The TV film, narrated by CBS correspondent Don Webster, showed a South Vietnamese soldier stabbing a prisoner to death.

Shortly thereafter the Pentagon requested the outtakes of the broadcast (film taken but not shown). CBS refused. The Pentagon seemingly lost interest in the case, but not Mollenhoff. In May 1970, he leaked a White House memo to columnist Richard Wilson (60 papers), a former colleague on the *Register and Tribune,* and to columnist Jack Anderson, partner and successor to the late Drew Pearson (600 papers). Both published stories alleging that the stabbing was merely a training exercise (the prisoner, according to this version, was already dead, and therefore legitimate practice material), and that CBS had staged the incident, just as it had staged "police brutality" at the 1968 National Democratic Convention in Chicago.

On May 21, soon after the leak—plant is a better word—Walter Cronkite in an unusual seven-minute segment of the CBS Evening News, said:

For reasons not entirely clear, the White House has engaged in an undercover campaign to discredit CBS News by alleging that the story was faked. . . . We broadcast the original story in the belief that it told something about the nature of the war in Vietnam. What has happened since tells us something about the government and its relations with news media which carry stories the government finds disagreeable.

Correspondent Webster on the same broadcast then offered a detailed refutation of the government's allegations, and named the South Vietnamese sergeant responsible for the stabbing. Then, in an interview with the sergeant, Webster elicited the admission that he had indeed stabbed a living man. The sergeant, who was later named "Soldier of the Year" by the government in Saigon, remembered the CBS-TV crew being present.

The White House made no direct charge against CBS, nor did it bring the matter to the attention of the Federal Communications Commission. Had it done so, CBS would have had a formal opportunity to defend itself. Immediately after the CBS broadcast of May 21, both the Pentagon and the White House disclaimed responsibility for the leaked memo. Herbert Klein, White House communications director (a new post instituted by the Nixon administration), according to a difficult-to-believe report in *Newsweek* magazine (June 1), did not know of the leak until CBS called him and advised him to tune in on Cronkite.

Ten days later, Mollenhoff announced his resignation from government service to become Washington bureau chief of the *Register and Tribune,* an offer "too good" to be turned down. Mollenhoff by this time had antagonized too many important persons inside and outside the Administration, and had become a liability. He had, in short, become too clumsy with his cocktails.

Cronkite was painfully correct in noting that the incident spoke volumes about the government. But what about columnists Wilson and Anderson, who printed Mollenhoff's concoction without checking with CBS? What about the other networks, who remained silent about the whole matter, and the newspapers whose lack of editorial comment was eloquent? And what, finally, about the television industry which, along with the rest of us, watches the slaughter in Southeast Asia nightly on its own screens, is aware of the integrity of its correspondents in the field—yet continues to support the American presence in Indochina as essential to the preservation of democracy in that area? End the war? Yes, eventually—but never on the only logical and moral terms possible—immediate agreement to withdraw American forces from all of Indochina. Not even CBS, whose forthrightness in defense of the truth was as commendable as it was rare in an industry not noted for spine.

"If it had just been a single episode," said Cronkite, "I think it could have been forgotten. But it represents a continuing attitude and a threat to all of us in the media." This assertion was underscored in a letter to CBS from Senator William Fulbright, chairman of the Senate Foreign Relations Committee, which was printed in *Variety*—and, to the best of my knowledge, in no newspaper of general circulation. Fulbright said:

Never before have our democratic institutions—whether the Congress or the free press—been so seriously threatened by an Administration experienced in the techniques of mass advertising, and uninhibited in presenting innacurate or misleading information in order to sell official policies. It is not by chance, I believe, that the Vice President's campaign of intimidation and criticism is now followed by specific attacks by the Administration upon specific television networks or newspapers on specific stories."

At times like these, Fulbright concluded, "the media must meet the responsibilities not just as reporters of favorable or unfavorable facts, but as responsible critics of policies."

How well have the media met these responsibilities? There has been some evidence of increasing defiance, but there has also been much backing and filling, and internal battles in the higher echelons of industry, indicating that there is still a long way to go before the communications industry comes fully awake to its responsibilities as watchdog of the public in the national interest.

12

What makes Spiro talk?

"I THINK the industry as a whole has been intimidated," said Cronkite of the combined Agnew-Mitchell assault on the media. Norman E. Isaacs, who was president of the American Society of Newspaper Editors at the time of the first Agnew speeches, said he had been buried under an avalanche of "sick mail," including remarks about the "Jew-owned and Jew-dominated news media." (Ironically, Isaacs was editor of the Louisville *Courier-Journal,* owned by the thoroughly WASP-ish Bingham family). Significantly, Isaacs said, half the mail from *editors* supported the Agnew position. He felt that Agnew's implied threat to the broadcast media had already succeeded.

In an interview with *Editor & Publisher* on August 22, 1970, John B. Oakes, editor of the editorial page of the *New York Times*, conceded that Agnew's speeches had affected him and the *Times*. He said that perhaps without realizing it, there had been a certain toning down, a hesitancy, or reluctance in the quality of the *Times's* dissent. The attitude of the Nixon Administration, he said, had uglier overtones than those of previous administrations which had reacted sharply to criticism.

The full ugliness of the Administration's intent was made apparent in a speech by Vice President Agnew in Houston on May 22, 1970. It produced this startled response from I. F. Stone in his *Bi-Weekly* of June 1: "When I began publication in the heyday of McCarthyism 18 years ago I never dreamed that someday I would share the pillory with a Luce publication! In journalism at least Nixon has kept his pledge and brought us all together."

It was no mean achievement for the nation's No. 1 polarizer to establish a union not only of Stone and Hugh Sidey of *Life*, but James Reston, Tom Wicker, and Anthony Lewis of the *New York Times* (one of the few papers to publish the Agnew speech in full), Herbert Block (Herblock) of the *Washington Post*, Harriet Van Horne and Pete Hamill of the *New York Post*, syndicated columnist Carl T. Rowan, and the *Atlanta Constitution* and the *Arkansas Gazette*.

Agnew's chief complaint was that the culprits had been critical of the invasion of Cambodia, and that some of them had described this action and the President's denigration of campus protesters as contributing factors in the death of four students at Kent State University. For all its familiarity, there was a new dimension to the speech that made it perhaps the most ominous portent yet from the White House regarding dissent.

The press was not Agnew's chief target in that speech, but rather a convenient vehicle to strike at a more persistent and consistent group of dissenters—the university students and faculty members whose unity in the aftermath of Cambodia, Kent, and Jackson State represented an immediate and direct threat to Administration policy. Agnew said:

> Those who would tear our country apart or try to bring down its government are enemies, whether here or abroad, whether destroying libraries and classrooms on a college campus or firing at American troops from a rice paddy in Southeast Asia. . . . They are a small, hard core of hell raisers who want to overturn the system for the sake of chaos alone. . . . They are encouraged by an equally small number of faculty members who apparently cannot compete legitimately within the system or do not choose to do so.
>
> It is my honest opinion that this hard core of faculty and students should be identified and dismissed from the otherwise healthy body of the college community lest they, like a cancer, destroy it.

The press, in Agnew's view, by criticising the President, encourages the spread of malignant dissent in the universities. With the "isolationists in the Senate" who "seek at every turn to thwart the President's efforts" to prevent a "Communist takeover" in Southeast Asia, and the "electronic media," they form an unholy trinity in the service of Satan (Communism) to destroy the American way of life.

Nixon and Agnew knew that the deepest-going dissent against Administration policy was not in the news media or in the Congress, but in the intellectual community. They knew also that the dissenting students and teachers were ranging out from the campuses seeking allies among union members, the poor, and the minorities in the inner cities. This was the motivation for the Hard Hat Uprising in New York, blessed by George Meany and anointed by Nixon, and it was the motivation for Agnew at Houston. The White House strategists felt that the time was not right for a confrontation with the university community, so the attack was indirect. This was the strategy:

First, seek to intimidate the news media away from giving space and voice to the new turn of dissent.

Second, discourage members of Congress from supporting the university community.

Third, if and when the first two missions are successful, come down hard on the dissenting students and faculty.

Meanwhile, the barrage must be maintained against dissent, whatever its degree, in every area of American life.

13

Stage-managing the news

It HAS become a cliche to say that all national administrations seek to manage the news. But the Nixon Administration may be recorded as the first to *stage-manage* the news. The strategy is carefully planned under the direction of communications coordinator Klein.

The process begins with the President himself and is modeled on the successful television campaign which packaged Nixon into a product just barely more acceptable to the electorate than Hubert H. Humphrey. Nixon has used television, both at press conferences and in special appearances unencumbered by the press, to a greater degree than any previous President to whom television was available. The use of television at press conferences tends to inhibit the already inhibited White House correspondents whose flabby questions, many of them planted in advance, have helped turn a once exciting event into a half-hour soporific.

Behind the scenes, however, a crisply rehearsed scenario is enacted, as described by a first-rate Washington correspondent, Jules Witcover of the *Los Angeles Times*.[10]

Klein regards the news media, as privately do most publishers and network officials, as a nationwide business. Unlike the media chiefs, however, he does not muffle his activities under a blanket of First Amendment platitudes. Where earlier Administrations transmitted their proposals and programs to the nation almost exclusively through the resident press corps in Washington (600 strong), the Klein formula is to go directly to the country itself—to the hundreds of daily newspapers and the thousands of television and radio stations.

The purpose of this approach is not to cut off the Washington press corps (which, with all its shortcomings, does to an extent strip the propaganda gloss off Administration releases), but rather to go beyond it and, in many cases, to preempt it. Thus, the President's speeches and the official explanations of his actions go immediately to the news editors and radio-TV stations throughout the country. They are followed up by briefing teams who visit with the news editors and publishers, wining and dining them at the best local establishments, flattering them with the impression that they have a direct pipeline to the White House. ("The President asked me particularly to tell you how much he enjoys reading your editorials . . . even though he may not always agree with them.")

The services of local public relations firms are engaged to smooth the way for the briefers, and the tab reportedly is picked up by the Republican National Committee. The guiding philosophy of this entire operation is the Spiro Agnew syndrome of distrust of the "Washington-New York news axis" and the "Eastern press" in general.

The President himself takes a hand by inviting regional editors and network officials to special briefings at Washington, or Chicago, or the West Coast White House, hard by the auto graveyards of San Clemente, California, and by making well-publicized visits to newspapers which support his policies. One such visit in the summer of 1970 was to the *Daily News* in New York. It was generally regarded as a deliberate snub to the *New York Times,* heretofore the holy mosque for all visiting dignitaries.

Although the *Daily News* meets Agnew's specifications for the "conglomerate category" (circulation two million, TV station and radio outlet in New York), it does not qualify for his abuse—because it is a loyal Nixon supporter. Actually, the *Daily News* is now under the control of the *Chicago Tribune,* which is one of the nation's giant conglomerates. The Tribune Company owns the afternoon daily *Chicago Today,* broadcast facilities in four states, cable television systems in two others, and newspapers in Florida.

The networks have not exactly thrown up barricades to halt this White House steamroller. Last May, for example, CBS refused to *sell* an hour's worth of time to Senators George McGovern and Mark Hatfield to present the case for the Church-Hatfield amendment designed to cut off funds for the Cambodian operation after a specific period of time—hardly a radical proposal. The hour was ultimately purchased from NBC for $70,000. Senator McGovern said: "I am puzzled by a communications policy that presents the President's side of the issue and won't even sell us time."

What a President has to say of course is news. For television the problem is somewhat different than for newspapers—aside from the fact that television stations depend for their existence upon licences issued by an agency of the Executive branch of government, the FCC. The President requests time, which is free, and at prime broadcast time, preempting profitable income time. In this way he commands television's "Page One" without competition.

A newspaper, on the other hand, can exercise some judgment in presenting the same speech or message by the President. While a newspaper almost invariably puts it on page one, it need not do so. Further, in the same edition, it can balance the news with comments from the President's critics. But television almost invariably waits until the 11 p.m. news broadcast, or even until the following day to present any criticism, and often then only in tepid fashion by network personnel, not by vigorous opponents of policy.

In this age of the mechanical making of a President, as was the case with Nixon, the skillful media manipulators in the White House take full advantage of this blend of newsprint tradition and electronic innovation. In the process they are helped immeasurably by media executives like Julian Goodman, president of NBC, who says he does not consider it proper for "political opponents" of the President to be interviewed immediately after he has spoken. Goodman found no impropriety in demanding and getting $70,000 cash from these same political opponents five days after the President's spoken word.

The White House attitude is supported also by the American Broadcasting Company network which, according to *Variety,* has designated a "happy news" producer, called by his sympathetic colleagues the "Agnews editor," because of Agnew's complaint that the media present only "bad news."

But the working press too is affected by the atmosphere of caution and crawl induced by the Administration's barrage against the media. A man who had been part of the government apparatus in one of its most powerful and obscured areas—the Pentagon—recently gave a frightening picture of this giant war machine at work, and what it gets away with. He is A. Ernest Fitzgerald, formerly an efficiency expert in the Defense Department, and later a consultant to the Businessmen's Educational Fund. In an article in *Variety,* he was quoted as presenting a panorama of vast cost overruns, of delivery of planes whose wings break off, tanks that blow themselves up, and "missiles that won't even make it out of their own silos."

Never has there been a greater need for thorough and objective reporting of the Pentagon, he said, because the Pentagon, "supposedly the main protector of our freedom, quite possibly is itself the greatest threat to our personal liberty." While acknowledging the difficulties in penetrating "the opaque shroud of secrecy" at the Pentagon, Fitzgerald recorded several instances in which networks have declined to pursue well-documented exposes of waste and dangerous inefficiency handed to them virtually on a silver platter. He cited specific stories, but not the names of the networks. *Variety* took up where he left off and filled in some of the names of those who rejected the material offered. Among them were the ABC network, and the Pentagon correspondent of CBS.

If the media, both in its top echelons and at the working press level, fail in their responsibility to expose this vast bureaucracy which controls the American military machine, there can hardly be any protection for the public which pays for this insanity with the lives of its sons and its earnings.

The CBS network finally consented late in June 1970 to offer free time, as a regular practice, to the principal political party not in the White House. This of course meant only the Democratic Party. The action came just as the Democrats were petitioning the FCC to force the networks to grant free equal time to opponents of the President's policies.

Thus it remained for the FCC to do what the networks themselves should have done long before. In August the FCC ruled that the networks were obliged to give prime time to critics of the President to respond to five televised speeches by the President about the war in Indochina.

Most news stories interpreted this decision to mean that the critics would henceforth get "equal time" on a regular basis. But Dean Burch, the former Goldwater aide who was appointed in 1969 by Nixon as chairman of the FCC, rushed in to charge the press with a mistaken interpretation. He declared that the FCC had "expressly rejected any principle embodying right of reply or rebuttal to the President." Burch had voted for the order, as had Commissioner Johnson, who took issue with Burch's interpretation. In a "clarification" of his position, Johnson said that comparable treatment to opposite views should be presented by the networks every time the President speaks. There was little doubt that Burch's hasty vehemence had been inspired by the White House, and with the new Nixon majority on the FCC the decision would be interpreted as the White House wished.

The FCC decision, although it represents a measure of progress, is severly restricted in scope by the limits of the major parties themselves. The views of the Democratic majority are not "opposite" to those of the Republican majority. They simply are a modification of Republican or national policy. The "opposite" view would have to come from the radical movement, and there is not even a suggestion of equal or comparable time for such a view. The airways, which belong "to the people," in practice belong to established power—in government and in the communications industry—which will neither permit nor sanction any extended presentation and discussion of views diametrically opposed to Administration policy—Republican or Democratic.

There was a vigorous demonstration of awareness of the dangers to a free press under the Nixon Administration in August 1970 in Washington. It came not from the media itself, however, but from university teachers. The Association for Education in Journalism, in a resolution approved by an overwhelming majority of the several hundred teachers present, condemned "in the strongest possible terms" the infringements on First Amendment freedom "being pursued under the leadership" of the White House. Nixon's name was specifically linked with Agnew's. In other actions, the association denounced the Administration for distorting information about the war in Indochina; for seeking to suppress discussion in the media about the war; for assembling secret dossiers on war reporters, and for employing spies posing as newspapermen.

The resolutions were heartening but they did not go far enough, as the teachers of journalism themselves probably discovered in their contact with some of the working editors in Washington. Several speakers from the press expressed the belief that Agnew was "right on target." Columnist James J. Kilpatrick said the charges of intimidation were "humbug." William Eaton of the *Chicago Daily News* saw nothing new in the Agnew attacks. Robert Phelps of the *New York Times* also felt the news corps was not intimidated. While the teachers' resolutions were accurate and appropriate, they would have been more effective if they had been directed not only at government but at the communications industry as well for its failure to live up to its own public assertions of independence.

14

Watching the watch dog

WHAT THEN can be suggested for a communications industry that seems to please no one, not government, nor the public, nor a large segment of the working staffs—in fact, no one apparently but the owners and operators of the industry? What changes can be proposed to instill a sense of responsibility in an industry—particularly the printed media—which has always been defensive of criticism from outside the industry, and entirely self-indulgent within the industry?

Until recently serious criticism has been remarkably lacking, except for some notable exceptions such as Upton Sinclair in his book, *The Brass Check,* now 50 years old, a bitter, documented indictment of the press; George Seldes's books of the 1930's and 1940's with bugle-call titles like *You Can't Print That!, Can These Things Be!,* and *Let the People Know;* and George Marion's *Stop the Press!* (1953), which more than the others of recent times placed the newspaper industry within the context of American monopoly capital.

There must be a special place for the late A. J. Liebling, whose evilly cheerful essays in the *New Yorker* magazine, subsequently in book form, comprised a most serious and penetrating indictment of the press and its coverage of important news events, Liebling, Seldes, and Marion (who for many years was on the staff of the *New York Mirror,* a

Hearst newspaper) were vigorous proponents of the American Newspaper Guild, founded in 1933.

There were sound economic reasons for a union of editorial and commercial employees in those Depression days. Payroll cuts and payless paydays were common, as were arbitrary firings. No thinking newspaperman rejected the economic reasons for the Guild (although some balked at rubbing elbows in meeting halls with ordinary clerks). But some hoped for something more than straight unionism, particularly those who had become disillusioned as a result of their experiences with the practice of freedom of the press, as opposed to the theoretical concept of the First Amendment. These newspapermen were persuaded that the Newspaper Guild had a responsibility that went far beyond the question of wages and hours and working conditions.

There was the matter of working on stories which they knew were being distorted after they left the typewriters of the reporters or the rewrite men. There was wire service copy which on its face was a fraud. Some publishers and editors favored certain politicians and advertisers in the news columns or, as on the Hearst newspapers, had a "Shit List" to guarantee that the listees never got favorable mention in the newspapers. What was the responsibility of a working newspaperman or woman in all of these things? After all, the press was the watch dog of the Republic in the public interest, and newspapers could not be published without the acquiescence and cooperation of the working press.

Such questions were not encouraged, even within the Guild. It was pointed out that the Guild was not an association of professional journalists. It was an industrial union of editorial workers, clerks, stenographers, maintenance men, and advertising solicitors. It would not be fair to them, the argument went, to raise questions about the content of newspapers. That was not the function of a union. Besides, the question of ownership was clear, and what went into a newspaper was the responsibility of the owner.

In default of the union of the working press, others inspected the performance, content, and responsibility of the press. The most pertinent and comprehensive report about the modern press was presented in 1947 as the Hutchins Commission Report, officially *A Free and Responsible Press: A General Report on Mass Communications: Newspapers, Radio, Motion Pictures, Magazines, and Books.* It was published by the University of Chicago, of which Robert M. Hutchins was then chancellor. The commission was made up of university experts, lawyers and industrialists, none of them identified with the left, and none involved with the communications media. The final report, drafted in October 1946, was described by James Boylan in the *Columbia Journalism Review* (Summer 1967) as "in a sense a postwar charter for the press." It remains so today, unread and unheeded, except at anniversary time by the professional publications of journalism.

The commission found that while the press had developed enormously as an instrument of mass communication, the proportion of people who could express their ideas and opinions through the press had decreased. Those in control not only had not provided a service adequate to the needs of society, but had even engaged in practices which society condemns. It listed five requirements of a press in a free society:

1. A truthful, comprehensive and intelligent account of the day's events in a context which should give them

meaning. . . . It is now necessary to report *the truth about the fact.*

2. A forum for the exchange of comment and criticism.

3. The projection of a representative picture of the constituent groups of society.

4. The presentation and clarification of the goals and values of society . . . clarifying the ideals toward which the community should strive.

5. Full access to the day's intelligence.

"One of the most effective ways of improving the press," the report said, "is blocked by the press itself: By a kind of unwritten law, the press ignores the errors and misrepresentations, the lies and scandals of which its members are guilty." It made several suggestions, one of which was unusually innovative and controversial:

We recommend the establishment of a new and independent agency to appraise and report annually on the performance of the press. In this field we cannot turn to government as representative of the people as a whole, and we would not do so if we could. Yet it seems clear that some agency which reflects the ambitions of the American people for its press should exist for the purpose of comparing the accomplishments of the press with the aspirations the people have for it. Such an agency would also educate the people as to the aspirations which they ought to have for the press.

When the report was released late in March 1947, the press reacted in classic fashion: it confirmed the commission's description of the press. Harry Ashmore, then editor of the *Arkansas Gazette,* recalled 20 years later: "I was a member of the American Society of Newspaper Editors when *A Free and Responsible Press* was published, and saw the august membership huddle rumps together, horns out, in the immemorial manner, say, of the National Association of Manufacturers faced by a threat of regulated prices."[11] A headline over a story about the report in the *Chicago Tribune* read: "A Free Press (Hitler style) Sought for U.S.; Totalitarians Tell How It Can Be Done."

Nearly a quarter century later, almost nothing of the commission's recommendations has been implemented. Newspapers have not notably concerned themselves with enlarging their horizons culturally or socially. Too many schools of journalism remain for the most part workshops divorced from the needs of society, or even devoid of an awareness that "society" exists somewhere outside. Radio, and now television, remain firmly in the control of advertisers, in many of whose firms television network board members hold shares. One major wire service and scores of newspapers have died. The government seeks constantly by means of the press to obfuscate its policies rather than present them clearly to the public, and the managers of newspapers generally allow their property to be thus abused because they support governmental policies.

Most significantly, no agency to evaluate and watch over the press has ever been established, and the general sessions of newspaper and broadcasting executives are almost devoid of mutual and meaningful criticism.

In the early 1960's, local press councils, comprising citizens from all areas of endeavor, were proposed. The plan was for them to meet with the local newspaper publisher or editor to exchange views toward creating a newspaper more responsive to the needs of the community. But it was not until 1967, when the Lowell Mellett Foundation helped to finance experimental projects, that the idea took hold. Councils were set up in small cities in California, Oregon, and Illinois. They reported mixed results. The main benefit was affording the community the means to confront publishers with needs and grievances; but genuine results depended on the receptivity of the newspaper publishers, and that was not wholehearted. Some councils were discontinued after the Mellett funds ran out. Others were continued with local funding.

The press council idea is a healthy one, and the reluctance of the overwhelming majority of publishers to encourage it indicates that they fear not so much an encroachment on freedom of the press as a watchful eye on their license to do whatever they want without accounting to the public they supposedly serve.

Nervous discussion within the industry offers evidence that the publishers know they are being watched. In 1969, the board of the American Society of Newspaper Editors held its annual meeting in London as a manifest of its interest in the council idea. They engaged in a comprehensive study of the national British Press Council, which has been credited—despite some severe criticism of its operations—with improving the standards of the British press.

But the ASNE group was reluctant to establish an American counterpart. The reasons given were the infinitely greater size of the United States, differences in judicial systems, concepts of ethics, and in public attitudes. The board went as far as to propose an ASNE Grievance Committee "to receive complaints in substance about the performance of daily newspapers." But the complaints would be restricted to those by one newspaper organization against another.

Interestingly enough, at the session of the journalism educators mentioned earlier, Norman

Isaacs, who was president of the ASNE at the time of the London meeting, advocated establishment of a press council similar to Britain's. Despite present opposition, he said, "we may have the beginnings of such an institution within four to five years."

15

Rebellion in the ranks

ISAACS MAY be right. The publishers and editors may agree, if only in self-defense, to the establishment of a council in whose formation they will have a large measure of control. But some in the industry were not willing to wait four to five years. They began in 1968 to form "press councils" within the industry, and even within individual publications to examine the performance of the press and their own role in it. They were not publishers and editors, but reporters and rewrite men, for the most part young and fairly new to the industry, but often acting with the sympathy and cooperation of more experienced colleagues who shared their exasperation.

The first striking demonstration of this disaffection took place in Chicago in the weeks following the Democratic National Convention in August 1968. Reporters and photographers who were liberally clubbed by the police, along with young demonstrators, suffered perhaps greater injuries to their integrity when they repaired to the supposed safety of their news rooms after the street scenes. There,

as one reporter said, "our own editors told us that
we didn't see what we really saw under those blue
helmets."

Angry and frustrated, the news men and women
formed an Assoication of Working Press, and
founded the *Chicago Journalism Review.* The stated
objectives, in addition to the right to cover the news
without interference by the police or other governmental agencies, were "to improve professional
standards of fairness and accuracy in the media;
publicly condemn obvious breaches of journalistic
ethics," and contribute to the continuing education
of the press corps through seminars, lectures, and
publications. The goals were remarkably similar to
those of the Hutchins Commission 21 years earlier.

Despite financial problems, the *Review* has been
remarkably effective in stirring the consciences of
news staffs in Chicago and throughout the country.
After two years, its circulation reached 7,000, much
of it outside Chicago. At first, the Chicago newspapers ignored its documented accounts of suppression of stories, censorship and unfair treatment
of personnel, kindly treatment of corporate business, and omissions in reporting on major events.
But in the first months of 1970, when the *Review*
began to reveal the outside interests and connec-
tions of Chicago's publishers, the newspapers began to strike back. This helped to spark a lively
debate about "objective" journalists versus "activist" journalists which spread through the newspapers of the country, and into the television networks. Even more significant were moves by staff
members of many publications toward a greater
voice in the editorial policy-making of their publications, and in the selection of editorial personnel,
particularly the editors themselves.

There were European models for this latter

thrust, mainly in France and in Western Germany, where staffs had engaged in strikes and the threat of strikes in successful efforts to achieve greater editorial control on the papers they helped to produce—for example, *Der Stern,* published in Hamburg, generally described as West Germany's *Life* magazine; *Le Figaro, L'Express,* and *Le Monde* in Paris. On its own, *Le Monde's* management had agreed to the formation within the staff of a society of editors and to an agreement giving the staff a 40 per cent share in the profits and a large share in the policy-making and managerial decisions, including the right to block any future sale of the paper. Similar societies have been set up on other European publications.

Tradition-bound publishers in the United States might be impressed with the results of the *Le Monde* experiment in shared management, as related in Jean Schwoebel's book (unfortunately thus far published only in French) entitled *Press, Power, and Money.* Under control of its editorial staff, *Le Monde* has achieved first rank in France, with a modern plant, and a profit in 1969 of $3.5 million on a gross income of $20 million. A key to its editorial excellence is the fact that it has turned down millions of dollars in advertising in order to maintain a 3-to-2 ratio of news to advertising.

In the United States, of course, no such situation exists as yet, and it is not likely to occur for some time to come. But the pressures for change are strong. Agreements have been reached at several publications for joint management-staff discussions on editorial policy, and in several cities publications like the *Chicago Journalism Review* were being published. Among the newspapers where management-staff discussions were being held are the *New York Post,* the Gannett newspapers in

Rochester, New York, the *Denver Post,* the *Journal* and the *Bulletin* in Providence, and the *Minneapolis Tribune,* where a *Twin Cities Journalism Review* was being planned.

In New York a monthly *Pac-O-Lies* began publication in 1969 and an *AP Review* was organized in 1970; *Point of View* was being published in Cleveland, and the *St. Louis Journalism Review* put out its first issue in September 1970. An Association of Public Television Producers also has been formed. The television journalists have become increasingly concerned with the unrestricted profit-making operations of commercial television, the politicians' grip on public television, and the danger that cable television (CATV), which will link even the remotest outposts of the country to the television centers of the nation, will fall almost completely under the control of the giant TV networks and the telephone and telegraph monopolies—as is already proving to be the case.

Parallel to the movement for greater editorial voice by the staffs has been the so-called activist movement. Editorial personnel, once bound by an unwritten code—and threat of reprisal—to evidence no personal feeling or political conviction, are taking an active position on politcal issues and participating in political and social protest movements. At the time of the Anti-War Moratorium on October 15, 1969, 308 members of the staff of the *New York Times* asked for and were refused the use of the Times Auditorium for a meeting. Outside the building 150 employees held a silent vigil and then marched to a publishing industry rally nearby. At *Time, Newsweek,* and the *Wall Street Journal,* management was confronted with petitions asking for an observance of Moratorium Day. The *Time* petition was signed by 462 staff members and moved management to grant the use of the auditorium for a meeting of 500 persons—including publisher Henry Luce III. At *Newsweek*, 250 employees failed to show up for work on October 15.

Associations of black journalists have come into being in the major newspaper centers to monitor the performance of publications on racial questions, to ensure fair treatment for black employees, and to pave the way for hiring of more black personnel. The impressive support given to Earl Caldwell of the *New York Times* in his subpoena fight was an overt demonstration of the potential power of these organizations.

The women's liberation movement has inspired increasing activity on the part of women editorial employees for upgrading their jobs (on the news magazines, for example, the overwhelming percentage of researchers are women, who are in turn notable for their absence among the reporting and writing personnel). There have been a sit-in at *McCall's* magazine and confrontations at the *New York Post* and at *Newsweek*, where the persistent efforts of women editorial personnel resulted in a firm agreement on management's part to guarantee equal treatment for women employees.

And the American Newspaper Guild, which almost since its founding has eschewed such questions as the contents of newspapers, the rights of newsmen and women in off-the-job activities, and ethical practices in the newsrooms, at its convention in 1970 passed several resolutions which brought it sharply into the midst of the changing newspaper scene. The *Guild Reporter,* the organ of the American Newspaper Guild, particularly in the first months of 1970, reflected this new awareness.

There has been of course strong opposition to some of the activist movements on the part of management, and this will continue. At the *Washington Post,* executive editor Benjamin Bradlee insisted that a reporter "must not only avoid emotional involvement, but the appearance of it. In other words, no armbands, no buttons." On the other hand, in the *Bulletin* of the American Society of Newspaper Editors February 1970 a far more sympathetic view was taken by Derick Daniels, executive editor of the *Detroit Free Press,* and Norman A. Cherniss, associate editor of the *Riverside* (California) *Press-Enterprise.*

Their theme was essentially the matter of objectivity in the news, the shibolleth which for generations has been the vehicle for countless news stories crucifying innocent persons and tarnishing the character of persons who had no access to the press to counter the "objective" stories written about them.

A classic case was the press treatment of Senator Joe McCarthy and his activities in the early 1950's. Under the code of "objective reporting," the press of the United States was largely instrumental in building McCarthy into the formidable figure he became. Even though the newsmen who covered McCarthy (they were a specially assigned group known as "the goon squad") knew McCarthy was a liar and a charlatan, and that his charges were almost 100 per cent baseless in fact, they declared that the strictures of objectivity forced them to report the Senator's charges without comment— unless they were rebutted by the person under attack or by a political opponent of McCarthy, who could then be quoted.

This of course was nonsense. If the reporters (and their editors) knew that the charges were false—and a minimum of digging would have documented their falseness—it was their obligation to publish the documentation. The victims were generally unavailable for comment or fearful of making a statement because of the likelihood of perjury charges in the poisoned atmosphere of the time. Informers abounded who would lie to support McCarthy's lies. A responsible press would have exerted every effort to help the victims set the record straight. But "objectivity" forbade this. It was, however, far more than this convenient catch phrase: it was prejudice and fear on the part of editors and, unfortunately, too many of the working press. The myth of the "international communist conspiracy" had taken hold in the ranks of the press, as well as in the general population.

16

Looking forward

THE ANTI-COMMUNIST mythology no longer has a grip on the working members of the communications industry. Too much has happened in the 1960's. The emergence of the militant black freedom movement, the young white radical movement, the rise of anti-war sentiment in labor's ranks, women's liberation, the disillusionment of the majority of young people with liberal politics in the traditional electoral sense, the revolt in the universities (not only in America but throughout the world), and above all, the war in Indochina—all these things have combined to break the effectiveness of the Cold-War mythology.

This is not to say that efforts to preserve it do not

go forward with the utmost intensity. The Cold-War mythology remains the driving force of the Nixon Administration, as it was the motivating force of every national administration since Harry Truman's. In the area of the press, it is demonstrated in its most blatant form in the activities of Vice President Agnew, Attorney General Mitchell, and the entire White House apparatus whose aim is to make the communications media even more an arm of government than it already is.

The resistance, as we have seen, stems mainly from the so-called alternative press—the political radical press and the underground press—and from the working staffs of newspapers and the television networks. The resistance is growing, as it is in many other areas of American professional life—law, medicine, the clergy, the social sciences—but it is not yet enough, and the counter-forces both within the communications industry and in government are strong and efficient.

The resistance is not helped nor the rebellion enhanced by the many parochial attitudes that prevail among radical groups, as reflected in the radical and underground press. Sectarianism has been a barrier to progress among radicals for generations, and the strident tone, lack of flexibility, and strictured language of the press of the young radical movement has helped to maintain these barriers— with all due respect for the fact that the radical point of view has been systematically left out or played down by the general media.

If genuine objectivity means that newspapers must present not only the facts, but the facts about the facts—that is, to report in depth about the causes of an event, and interpret the event and its causes in the fairest possible manner—than the radical press too must be faulted. Its credibility must come into question along with that of the commercial press if it presents lopsided news and analysis which is accepted and approved only by a narrow circle of the faithful.

It may produce a snicker in some circles to have America spelled with a K rather than a C. But it is at bottom an excercise in adolescent semantics. It may produce a certain elation in some groups to say "off the pig," and there may be validity in this elation, but it is not in the vocabulary of 99 per cent of the population. And even at that, some cops are young, black, and even human. Thus, to class them all permanently as porkers may be both a political and sociological error. A documented article with cogent argument, written in language which is clear and understandable to all readers, is far more effective than a three- or four-letter word, or the use of the letter K.

In essence, any newspaper—radical or otherwise—must be a newspaper first and a political entity second. If a radical newspaper seeks to influence the public, it must maintain flexibility without yielding on principle. Until the radical movement can resolve its internal differences and relax its tension points, its publications will reflect these divisive factors to the point where they will largely be ineffective within the radical movement, and therefore almost totally ineffective among the general public. And surely they will suffer from a credibility gap.

There is a possibility of self-criticism and self-imposed reform in the radical press, and it is to be devoutly hoped that it will become a general practice. There is almost no possibility that such self-inspection will take place in the near future among the managers of the communications industry. Yet there is room for optimism. The ferment within the industry and the aspirations of the young journalists there cannot be discouraged. Because the press enjoys unique constitutional privileges and protections which give it special responsibilities, the rebellion in the ranks will be enormously important in forcing the owners to give something more than lip service to these responsibilities.

The rebellion has no easy chance of success, but it must be pursued if there is ever to be a fundamental change in American journalism. If the rebellion succeeds, the education of the American public as to the overriding importance of a truly free and responsible press may be achieved largely within the industry. If the movement is blocked, it will continue outside the industry to develop an alternative press—this time, I believe, with the collaboration of highly skilled journalists who will be departing in frustration from the establishment press.

The most heartening fact of American journalism in the decade of the 1970's is that there is in the United States a company of honest journalists of all ages, conscious of their own responsibility as journalists and human beings both, conscious of the potential power of an informed people, who will never give up the effort to establish an honorable and constructive communications network.

That is the hope of the future of American journalism.

Reference notes

1. *American Journalism,* by Frank Luther Mott, the Macmillan Co., 1962.

2. Statistics of the Bureau of Advertising of the American Newspaper Publishers Association.

3. "The Black Press in Transition," by L. F. Palmer Jr., *Columbia Journalism Review,* Spring 1970.

4. Same as above.

5. *The Bending Cross,* by Ray Ginger, Rutgers University Press, 1949.

6. Gaye Sandler Smith in the *International Press Institute Report* (3-1969).

7. "The Press and the Bay of Pigs," by Victor Bernstein and Jesse Gordon, Columbia University Forum, Fall 1967.

8. "A Footnote to History: The Press and National Security," an address by Clifton Daniel, managing editor of the *New York Times,* at the World Press Institute, Macalester College, St. Paul, Minnesota, June 1, 1966.

9. From *Dateline 1966: Covering the War,* published by the Overseas Press Club.

10. "The Two Hats of Herbert Klein," by Jules Witcover, *Columbia Journalism Review,* Spring 1970.

11. Harry S. Ashmore in the *Columbia Journalism Review,* Summer 1967.

Recommended reading

American Journalism, by Frank Luther Mott (Macmillan, 1962), recently revised, the most complete and accurate history written.

The Compact History of the American Newspaper, by John Tebbell (Hawthorn, 1963), a short, readable, and often pungent survey.

Reporting the News, edited by Louis M. Lyons (Harvard University Press, 1965), 51 articles on journalism from the magazine of the Nieman Fellows, with an introduction by Lyons, the founding curator.

The Adversaries, by William Rivers (Beacon, 1970), selected essays by working correspondents and graduate students on politics and the press.

The Information War, by Dale Minor (Hawthorn, 1970), conflict between the communications media and government, with stress on radio coverage.

How to Talk Back to Your Television Set, by Nicholas Johnson (Atlantic-Little Brown, 1970), sharp comment by the most outspoken member of the Federal Communications Commission.

Anything But the Truth, by William McGaffin and Erwin Knoll (Putnam, 1968), how the government seeks to manage the news.

The Making of A Quagmire, by David Halberstam (Random House, 1965), the battle of a *New York Times* reporter in Vietnam with government—American and South Vietnamese.

The Second Indochina War, by Wilfred Burchett (International, 1970), the truth about Cambodia and Laos, by the most informed reporter in Southeast Asia.

The Press, by A. J. Liebling (Ballatine Books, 1961), classic essays on the performance of the modern American press.

The Press and the Cold War, by James Aronson (Bobbs-Merrill, 1970), a documented study on the degree to which the press has become a voluntary arm of government.

The Kingdom and the Power, by Gay Talese (World, 1969), a vivid rendition of the personalities at work in the *Times* empire.

Due to Circumstances Beyond Our Control, by Fred Friendly (Random House, 1967), the fight for good documentary telecasting by the former head of CBS-TV News.

The Press and Foreign Policy, by Bernard C. Cohen (Princeton University Press, 1963), the relationship and the problems inherent in the making and reporting of foreign policy.

Never Tire of Protesting, by George Seldes (Lyle Stuart, 1968), a summing up of a career by a pioneer muck-raker in the field of journalism.

Communications Control, edited by John Phelan S. J. (Sheed & Ward, 1969), readings in the motives and structures of censorship.

Mass Communications and American Empire, by Herbert Schiller (Augustus M. Kelley, 1969), a comprehensive study of the structure and policy of mass communications in relation to their economic and political functions.

Truth Is the First Casualty, by Joseph C. Goulden (Rand McNally, 1969), a compelling study of the illusion and reality of the Gulf of Tonkin affair, a turning point in Vietnam.

The Hidden History of the Korean War, by I. F. Stone (Monthly Review Press, 1969), the facts about a grossly misinterpreted and crucial era in the history of American foreign policy.

The Autobiography of Lincoln Steffens (Harcourt, Brace, 1931), the document of a great life by one of American journalism's great crusaders for truth in the news.

ABOUT THE AUTHOR

A graduate of Harvard College and the Columbia Graduate School of Journalism, James Aronson has had extensive journalistic experience on both the Establishment and Radical press. He was on the staff of the *New York Times,* the *Herald Tribune* and the *Post* of New York City, and the Boston *Evening Transcript.* He then became a co-founder, and for many years editor, of the *National Guardian,* until he left to begin a new career as an author and teacher of journalism at New York University and the New School for Social Research. He is the author of *The Press and the Cold War* (Bobbs-Merrill, 1970), a study of the degree to which the press has become an arm of government. Another book, tentatively called *Rebellion in the Media,* will be published by Bobbs-Merrill in the fall of 1971. He writes a regular commentary on the media for *Antioch Review* and is a frequent contributor to liberal and radical journals. He is editor of the bi-monthly *Rights,* of the National Emergency Civil Liberties Committee. He lives with his wife, Grambs Miller, an artist and illustrator, in Manhattan's East Vilage.